Eight Mansions
FENG SHUI

Moon Gate Press
Houston, Texas

*This book is dedicated to my little Tiger,
Grayson*

Eight Mansions Zodiac Feng Shui
Copyright© 2021 by Denise A. Liotta-Dennis
First Edition, First Printing

Photography & Illustrations
Illustrations and charts created by Denise Liotta Dennis. Photos provided by Unsplash Pixabay. Credit and thanks to the following photographers Jackson Sackey, Jackson David, demarius, thwangfsdesign, Rizal Deathrasler, Anvatasia Gepp, Pera Deflic, Bessi, Leroy Skalstad, Shwrypa, Beton Ethemi, Cong-DucNguyen, Amber Clay, Benjamin, Blazs, Harpreet Batish, Songjayjay, ibuTuma, Dayron Villaverde, Bobby McIntye, Shahid Shafiq, pankajarnob, and diyprojects, Cover/Book Designer: Denise Liotta Dennis; front cover photo by pixy.org

Notice of Rights
All rights reserved. No part of this publication may be reproduced, stored in a retrieval system or transmitted in any form, or by any means, electronic, mechanical, photocopying, recording, or otherwise, without the written permission of the publisher. For reprints and excerpts, contact: denise@dragongatefengshui.com

Notice of Liability
The information in this book is distributed on an 'as is" basis, without warranty. While every precaution has been taken in the preparation of the book, neither the author nor Moon Gate Press shall have any liability to any person or entity with respect to any loss or damaged caused or alleged to be causes directly or indirectly by the instructions contained in this book. The moral right of the author has been asserted.

Published by Moon Gate Press (713-897-1719) and Kindle Direct Publishing/Create Space

ISBN: 9798559412320
Published in the United States of America
Jan 2021

Table of Contents

INTRODUCTION 5

CHAPTER 1: BaZhai Secrets 7

CHAPTER 2: The Eight Life-Gua Numbers 11

CHAPTER 3: Eight Life-Guas + 5 Elements 25

CHAPTER 4: The 12 Chinese Zodiac Animals 28

CHAPTER 5: Life-Gua Zodiac Personalities 39

CHAPTER 6: The 64 Compatibilities 157

CHAPTER 7: Workplace and Career 194

CHAPTER 8: Applications for Home & Office 204

GLOSSARY OF TERMS 215
AUTHOR'S BIO 229
COMPASS READINGS 233

INTRODUCTION

I'm very excited to bring you a book that has a fresh perspective on the famous Chinese Zodiac and the powerful Eight Mansions (BaZhai) style of Feng Shui together in one place.

Eight Mansions is likely the second most popular system in Classical Feng Shui after Flying Stars. They both can have a powerful affect on your everyday life. I learned Eight Mansions directly from Grandmaster Yap Cheng Hai. He was brought to the world's attention by Lillian Too. She consulted him on her first few books including *Applied Pa Kua and Luo Shu Feng Shui* published in 1993. This was the first book in English about the Eight Mansions system. Up until that time, most Westerners had never heard of this simple, powerful system that can produce profound results.

Classical Feng Shui makes extensive use of the 12 Animals of the Chinese Zodiac. They are used as markers of time. The animals are assigned specific types of energy that gives us clues into what motivates people born in those years. The 12 Animals of the Chinese Zodiac are also part of important trines of energy which will indicate possible events, on the macro and micro level, for the year.

By putting it altogether, this book will give you some wonderful insider information about all your relationships, how to improve them and analyze them to your benefit. In ancient times, many cultures believe deeply in arranged marriages and they used many forms of astrology to compare the compatibility. Even the simple *Six Animal Clashes* can give insights into compatibility. Thankfully, nowadays an arranged marriage is not a practical approach. However, exploring compatibility is still very useful.

In addition to learning more about the 12 Animals of the Chinese Zodiac, you will learn about the Life-Gua Number in Eight Mansions. This number is highly significant for several reasons. Not only will this number tell you the best directions to activate in your home or office, you will be amazed at the 56 *Life-Gua Zodiac Personalities.* This is where the Life-Gua is matched up with the animal year of your birth. This will give you a better insight, not only for yourself, but others in your sphere.

There are also 64-Compatabilites where each of the 8 Life-Guas combines with each other. The focus here is primarily for examining harmony in romance and marriages. There is a wealth of information regarding the workplace in Chapter 7. Learn who will make the best employees, good work companions, who may try to control you, who may try to smash your ideas and much, much more. This is an invaluable tool to use before committing to a business partnership as well.

And finally in the last chapter we show you how to best set up your home or office using simple principles of Eight Mansions. Now let's dive right into the many gifts of Eight Mansions.

CHAPTER ONE
BaZhai Secrets

Chinese astrology, Feng Shui and astronomy are very ancient indeed and date back thousands of years. All were used by emperors and ordinary folks alike who sought insights into life's mysteries.

The focus of this book is to use Eight Mansions (BaZhai) Feng Shui system combined with and the 12 Animals of the Chinese Zodiac for a more comprehensive experience. Let's start with some a little background into Eight Mansions.

Eight Mansions, *BaZhai* in Chinese, is a Feng Shui system that is direct and simple. When applied correctly, many people have defeated serious problems concerning family, career, relationships, marriage, health and children. This was simply done by applying the principles of Eight Mansion using good directions and re-orienting specific rooms in their homes. In the last chapter we show you how to effectively apply the principles.

But it has other exciting aspects as well. For example, how to get a deeper understanding of the interaction with family members, partners in life (husbands and wives), children, lovers, friends and those people we work with such as co-workers, bosses, clients and students.

Before you can drastically improve your life at home and the workplace, you will need to determined your Life Gua number. Some masters call this number the Ming Gua or the Magic Gua Number. According to this Feng Shui system, based on your birthday and gender, you will be influenced in positive and negative ways by the eight directions: four will support you and four won't. The lucky directions will augment wealth and money luck, health, good relationships, and stability; the other four can set into motion divorce, bankruptcy, betrayals, lawsuits, cancer, and so forth. The idea is to use and activate your good directions and diminish the negative ones.

The Eight Mansions system dates back to the Tang Dynasty. While there were several popular styles back in the day, there were two that survived to present. They are the Eight House Bright Mirror and the Golden Star Classic.

In general, the two most popular systems of Feng Shui for the interiors of homes/buildings, is Eight Mansions and Flying Stars. While Eight Mansions is not as complex as Flying Stars, it is amazing. The Eight Mansions system's focus is on the *people* aspect, while Flying Stars' on the *structure*.

And the best news is when the Eight Mansions formula is applied correctly, it can bring dazzling prospects for love and romance, business opportunities, health, promotions at work, flourishing investments and money-luck. It can help identify negative energy, which will be apparent when people suffer from disease, poor health, a crippling divorce, bad relationships, accidents, disastrous events and bankruptcy. In addition, it is the *only* system which has a 'personality type' aspects. which is extremely useful for home and working relationships. We will delve deeper into the personality aspects in other chapters. Classical Feng Shui systems, including Eight Mansions, are all compass-based methods. Which means you'll need to take a compass direction of certain things in your space. This is why compass-based methods are more powerful than the one-size-fits-all types—they are accurate and specific to you and your unique space.

In order to really shake up the chi and get the life you want, you must be open minded to the fact that direction will influence your luck and opportunities. It may not sound logical, but by nature, Feng Shui is a metaphysical science. So, if you want to change things for the better, relax into the idea that you'll be arranging your space using specific degrees and directions.

As I mentioned in the introduction, the first book to introduce Eight Mansions to the public was *Applied Pa-Kua and Lo Shu Feng Shui* by Lillian Too in collaboration with Grandmaster Yap Cheng Hai (my teacher); this was in 1993. In this book, the author retells the story of how Master Yap spent three years unlocking the secrets from a tattered, antique manual.

This book was copied from a volume originally written during the Chien Lung period (1711-1799) of the Chin Dynasty by a Feng Shui Master from Southern China. While studying with Master Yap, he told his students many times, how fortunate he was to have received several, handwritten original texts from his four teachers and he treasured them greatly. Master Yap used the *Golden Star Classic* (Jin Guang Dou Lin Jing) style of Eight Mansions and was a huge fan of this system.

However, he practiced it much differently than other masters. It was the first formula he taught in his world-famous classes.
He would humorously demonstrate the power of Eight Mansions and bring the point home by saying:

"How are you going to help the homeless person on the street, change his bed or door? He doesn't have a door! But if you have him sleep to his best

direction, maybe someone will come along and offer him a job".

Eight Mansions Facets:

*The Life-Gua Numbers
East-West Life Groups
4 Good and 4 Bad Directions Advanced
Eight Mansions
8 Personality types*

CHAPTER TWO
The Eight Life-Gua Numbers

Remember, according to the Eight Mansions system, you will be influenced in positive and negative ways by the eight directions: four will support you and four won't. The lucky directions will augment wealth and money luck, health, good relationships, and stability. The other four can set into motion divorce, bankruptcy, betrayals, lawsuits, cancer, and so forth. The idea is to use and activate your good directions and diminish the negative ones. Before you can begin using this great system, you will need to determine your personal Life-Gua number.

To find your personal Life-Gua number, refer to Eight Mansions chart on the next page. Make sure you are in the right column as there is one for males and one for females. There is a specific calculation to arrive at this number, but I've included the quick reference chart for ease.

If you were born *prior* to February 4th in any given year, please refer to the previous year. For example, if you were born January 28, 1970, use the previous year 1969 to find the correct Life Gua number. Also, make note of the animal year of your birth; this is very important in our more inclusive examination of the Life-Gua +Zodiac Animal.

Locate Your Life-Gua Number

1933-1963

Animal	Year	Male ♂	Female ♀
Rooster	1933	4	2
Dog	1934	3	3
Pig	1935	2	4
Rat	1936	1	8
Ox	1937	9	6
Tiger	1938	8	7
Rabbit	1939	7	8
Dragon	1940	6	9
Snake	1941	2	1
Horse	1942	4	2
Goat	1943	3	3
Monkey	1944	2	4
Rooster	1945	1	8
Dog	1946	9	6
Pig	1947	8	7
Rat	1948	7	8
Ox	1949	6	9
Tiger	1950	2	1
Rabbit	1951	4	2
Dragon	1952	3	3
Snake	1953	2	4
Horse	1954	1	8
Goat	1955	9	6
Monkey	1956	8	7
Rooster	1957	7	8
Dog	1958	6	9
Pig	1959	2	1
Rat	1960	4	2
Ox	1961	3	3
Tiger	1962	2	4
Rabbit	1963	1	8

1964-1994

Animal	Year	Male ♂	Female ♀
Dragon	1964	9	6
Snake	1965	8	7
Horse	1966	7	8
Goat	1967	6	9
Monkey	1968	2	1
Rooster	1969	4	2
Dog	1970	3	3
Pig	1971	2	4
Rat	1972	1	8
Ox	1973	9	6
Tiger	1974	8	7
Rabbit	1975	7	8
Dragon	1976	6	9
Snake	1977	2	1
Horse	1978	4	2
Goat	1979	3	3
Monkey	1980	2	4
Rooster	1981	1	8
Dog	1982	9	6
Pig	1983	8	7
Rat	1984	7	8
Ox	1985	6	9
Tiger	1986	2	1
Rabbit	1987	4	2
Dragon	1988	3	3
Snake	1989	2	4
Horse	1990	1	8
Goat	1991	9	6
Monkey	1992	8	7
Rooster	1993	7	8
Dog	1994	6	9

1995-2025

Animal	Year	Male ♂	Female ♀
Pig	1995	2	1
Rat	1996	4	2
Ox	1997	3	3
Tiger	1998	2	4
Rabbit	1999	1	8
Dragon	2000	9	6
Snake	2001	8	7
Horse	2002	7	8
Goat	2003	6	9
Monkey	2004	2	1
Rooster	2005	4	2
Dog	2006	3	3
Pig	2007	2	4
Rat	2008	1	8
Ox	2009	9	6
Tiger	2010	8	7
Rabbit	2011	7	8
Dragon	2012	6	9
Snake	2013	2	1
Horse	2014	4	2
Goat	2015	3	3
Monkey	2016	2	4
Rooster	2017	1	8
Dog	2018	9	6
Pig	2019	8	7
Rat	2020	7	8
Ox	2021	6	9
Tiger	2022	2	1
Rabbit	2023	4	2
Dragon	2024	3	3
Snake	2025	2	4

Eight Mansions
Good and Bad Directions

		EAST Life Group			
		1	3	4	9
GMY:	Indications:				
+90	Wealth	SE	S	N	E
+80	Health	E	N	S	SE
+70	Relationships	S	SE	E	N
+60	Stability	N	E	SE	S
-60	Setbacks	W	SW	NW	NE
-70	Lawsuits/Affairs	NE	NW	SW	W
-80	Sickness	NW	NE	W	SW
-90	Disasters	SW	W	NE	NW

		WEST Life Group			
		2	6	7	8
GMY:	Indications:				
+90	Wealth	NE	W	NW	SW
+80	Health	W	NE	SW	NW
+70	Relationships	NW	SW	NE	W
+60	Stability	SW	NW	W	NE
-60	Setbacks	E	SE	N	S
-70	Lawsuits/Affairs	SE	E	S	N
-80	Sickness	S	N	SE	E
-90	Disasters	N	S	E	SE

Life Groups and GMY Codes

Now that you have your personal Life-Gua number, let's examine the charts on page 13, as it contains a good deal of information. First, based on your Life Gua number, you will be part of the *East Life Group* or the *West Life Group*. Those who are a 1, 3, 4 or 9 Guas are part of the East group, and those who are a 2, 6, 7, or 8 belong to the West group. As opposites attract, it's not unusual for couples to belong to a different group.

Next, notice the GMY Code column; this is the clever creation of my teacher Grandmaster Yap Cheng Hai to refer to your good and bad directions without using the Chinese words associated with them. For example your best direction will be +90 which indicate prosperity or wealth luck. The +80 will help you to secure vital health. The +70 direction is your personal direction to enhance romance, relationships and harmony and so forth. Once you have located your personal Life Gua number on the chart, just follow down that column to see all good and bad directions and a brief description of what they'll indicate if you use them. On page 16-17, you'll see the full descriptions and indications.

The Life-Gua number is highly significant, not only can you derive the directions that support you, but get important clues about your personality. It's also used to determine the capability of spouses, the relationship between parents and children, the dynamic between siblings, work mates and business partners. In Chapter Five, we will explore these exciting aspects.

Eight Mansions Descriptions

The detailed descriptions for the Eight Mansions system and what your good and bad directions could indicate are discussed below. Each of your auspicious directions will attract a slightly different kind of good luck to you.

When you *activate* a direction, you're actually facing that direction, whether you're at your desk, sitting in a chair, sleeping in your bed, or walking through a certain door on a regular basis. Doors are important in Feng Shui—naturally you'll want your front door facing one of your four good directions.

The Four Best Directions

***Sheng Chi* (+90)—Wealth**: Sheng Chi means 'generating breath' or energy that gives life. This is the number one direction to stimulate wealth. Often referred to as the *millionaire chi*, this direction is one that is good for business opportunities, promotions at work, descendants, and wealth-luck. Your Sheng Chi direction will also establish positions of authority and powerful connections.

***Tien Yi* (+80)—Health**: Tien Yi means the *heavenly doctor*, and this is the best direction to ensure good health. This direction also has been known to bring unexpected wealth, as if from the heavens. Using this direction can bring long life, close friends, excellent social standing and the power of speech.

***Yen Nien* (+70)—Relationships**: This direction is all about personal relationships, love of family, romantic partners, networking, and family harmony in general. If this direction is used it can bring well-to-do, famous and rich descendants. If you want to have children quickly, place your bed to this direction. The Yen Nien direction also connotes health and longevity.

***Fu Wei* (+60)—Stability**: This direction is a mirror of your own energy, and can bring stability. It connotes moderate wealth and happiness; it is a good alternative if you cannot use your best directions. The Fu Wei direction suggests a family that is middle-class with good harmony. If you want older children to move out of the house, use this direction.

The Four Worst Directions:

***Wo Hai* (-60)—Set-Backs**: If this direction is used, it will attract all sorts of aggravating obstacles, persistent set-backs, and losing money in investments. It can bring small disasters, but not overwhelming ones; nothing goes smoothly. For example, you may win your court case, but not receive the monetary settlement.

***Wu Gwei* (-70)—Lawsuits, Affairs & Betrayals**: This direction is referred to as the *five ghosts,* and it primarily indicates lawsuits and litigation. If you use this direction it can bring lots of trouble in romance, rebellious children, drug use, petty people, robberies, illicit affairs, hot-tempered people, betrayals, lack of support by employees, gossip and being undermined.

***Liu Sha* (-80)—Backstabbing, Accidents and Bad Health**: Known as the *six killing* direction; utilizing this direction will attract injury, loss of wealth, backstabbing, affairs, awful money luck, harm to you and the family, betrayals in business, accidents of all sorts, and serious illness such as cancer. The Liu Sha direction can have you become *unrecognized* in the world.

***Chueh Ming* (-90)—Total Disaster & Major Losses**: Activating this direction can bring grievous harm that may include bankruptcy, a death in the family, divorce, horrific failure in business, accidents and no descendants. It brings total disaster and major losses and should be avoided.

Eight Life-Gua Personality Types

As I mentioned earlier, in addition to having good and bad directions, you're assigned particular personality traits based on your Life-Gua number. Here you'll find general descriptions of the eight Life Guas *(Life Gua Personalities)*, then more detailed ones matched with the 12 Animals of the Chinese Zodiac (*Life-Gua Zodiac Personalities*) in Chapter 5 and finally comparing all the Life-Guas with each other (*Life-Gua Compatibility*) in Chapter 6.

Although the Life-Gua Personalities cannot be found in the ancient classic texts, the information on the Guas can. The idea started when Master Yap gave us quick, verbal description of each of the Life Guas' propensities in class one day in Cologne, Germany (2000). We were greatly entertained by this and I began sharing the descriptions when consulting with my clients giving them key information about their spouses, children, co-workers, business partners, bosses and family members. I also started including it in my training classes and public lectures; people loved it! It gives some very interesting insights into personalities, and clients have confirmed their accuracy. After many years of doing this verbally and informally, I decided to expand on Master Yap's three-word description of the Life-Guas and pen it. This was based on the extensive information available on the Guas, the five element theory, and the Tan Lang Stars (the 9 Stars) which share roots with this system.

In the descriptions you will see the good and bad. Please keep in mind that everyone is capable of exhibiting their negative aspects. We all have times we are not 'on'. Don't focus on the negative, you may already have evolved past most of it. The following are the *general* personality traits of the eight Guas. It is much like astrology when we refer to people as being a Gemini, Aries, Scorpio and so forth. *The Complete Idiot's Guide to Feng Shui* also features this personality aspect of Eight Mansions, albeit not as detailed as the descriptions you'll find in this book.

The East Life Group
1, 3, 4 and 9

1 Life Gua Personality (Water Energy): The 1 Gua's are highly intellectual and can be studious or even scholarly. To the outside world, they appear calm and cool, however inside they have a rich emotional makeup. As a result, at times they can be over emotional, moody, anxious and high strung. They are full of brilliant ideas and concepts, and are usually very good at making and holding onto money. The 1 Gua's are skilled at sizing up people using their natural, intuitive abilities. Since their element is water, they can be hard to pin down. They are sensual and can be highly sexual. Tending to keep secrets below the surface, 1 Guas are known to have secret lives.

3 Life Gua Personality (Big Wood Energy): Three Guas are extremely enterprising and have progressive ideas. They tend to be outspoken, direct, and organized. The 3 Gua's nature is one of nervousness punctuated by lots of energy and steam. Constantly crafting new inventions, new ventures or the latest thing, they love new beginnings and 'start ups'. When in a negative energy, the 3 Guas tend to self-punish, spread their energy too thin leading to collapse, and can be abrasive. However, they are full of surprises, 3 Guas have a sense of vitality and vigor that can overwhelm people.

4 Life Gua Personality (Small Wood Energy): Malleable, flexible, indecisive, the' 4 Gua's may 'blow with the wind' if not grounded, finding it hard to take a stand. In general, they usually are attractive people or may have movie-star qualities. The 4 Gua's are more prone to be sexually controlled by their partners than other Guas. They have progressive ideas and can become famous in writing or rich in the publishing business. The un-evolved 4's may self-destruct by refusing good advice. The 4 Gua's can somewhat remote and private, but they are also gentle people with an innocent purity.

9 Life Gua Personality (Fire Energy): 9 Guas have a sharp, brilliant intellect; they can also be wise, loyal, and sentimental. Blessed with a fiery spirit and energy, these Guas have a decided adventurous streak. The female 9's are usually beautiful like a diva or goddess but can be argumentative, aggressive, and rash. With concentrated and focused effort, they can reach great height of achievements and standing in the world. The truly un-evolved 9 Guas will exhibit mental illness such as paranoia and psychotic, unstable behavior. When grounded and evolved, the 9's can light up a room with their radiant energy!

The West Life Group
2, 6, 7, and 8

2 Life Gua Personality (Mother Earth Energy): The 2 Gua's exhibit persistence, dependability, and a calm demeanour. They can also be nurturing and supportive to their inner circle. With their calm, relaxed demeanors, 2 Guas are dependable and tend to have developed psychic abilities. They make excellent doctors or practitioners of alternate healing arts such as *chiropractry,* massage therapy, and acupuncture. Since the 2 Guas have the most yin energy of the Guas, they enjoy and feel comfortable in dark spaces, but have a tendency to depression or dark moodiness. Good spelunkers, these grounded people relish activities that focus on the earth—gardening, farming, construction, and agriculture.

6 Life Gua Personality (Big Metal Energy): The 6 Guas can easily step into positions of power and authority as they are natural leaders that seem to be blessed by the heavens. They make excellent lawyers, judges and CEO's as their energy commands respect. The 6 Gua's have a regal, royal air that is naturally unpretentious. Clear thinkers, lots of courage, possessing foresight, extremely creative, and they can hold their own in a debate. They need time alone as they often get caught up in over-thinking, which can lead to being sleep-deprived. Oozing with creativity, the 6 Guas are filled with ideas that involve large groups of people, a community or an organization.

7 Life Gua Personality (Small Metal Energy): 7 Guas tend to be youthful in behavior or appearance. They are very attracted to metaphysical studies and arts; they can be talkative, lively, and nervous. The 7 female Guas are often blessed with very good looks, and sensuous beauty. Comfortable with a lot of 'stage', the 7 Gua's are good at acting, speaking, in front of the camera or on the radio. With a strong tendency to over indulge in the pleasures of life such as food, drink, money, and sex, they must keep a balanced life. They can be a fast-talker, smooth talker, or have a razor-sharp tongue. The 7 Guas are very social, charming, and charismatic; they create stimulating, informative conversation wherever they go.

8 Life Gua Personality (Mountain Earth Energy): The 8 Guas have a stubborn, dependable and steadfast nature. They tend to have a great deal of integrity and are vey attracted to all things spiritual. They can become spiritual seekers, and trek the mountains in search of 'answers' and to find themselves. Hardworking and loving things of the earth, the 8's are talented in construction, real estate, and landscaping. They also have a little of 'save the world' energy. While the 8 Guas tend to resist change, they can deftly handle trouble without falling apart. Un-evolved 8 Guas can become hoarders, self-righteous and short-tempered. They are geared for success and often become very rich with worldly honors, recognition and status.

Advanced Eight Mansions

What happens if my partner and I belong to different Life Groups? Actually, this happens all the time; opposites attract. However, there is a solution. The Eight Mansions system has another level, *Advanced Eight Mansions* (AEM), which is used to assist couples belonging to opposite groups. Basic Eight Mansions is used to determine your Life-Gua Number, good/bad directions, and personality type.

In order to have the Feng Shui support both people, you'll have to use Advanced Eight Mansions for fine-tuning a desirable direction. This is really important in the 'shared space' (the bed). AEM allows certain 15 degree increments of your 'bad' directions to be used. This is how it works: the South is a bad direction for anyone who is West Life Group (2, 6, 7 or 8), but in AEM the first and third 15 degree of South can be used. Which means you can face your bed direction, desk or use doors facing these increments.

If you are East Life Group (1, 3, 4 or 9), the West is one of your bad directions. However, in AEM you can use the first and third 15 degree increments. Now having said that, the entire 45 degrees of North cannot be used by anyone who is part of the West Life Group (2, 6, 7 or 8), unfortunately, not one single degree. Notice the '24 Mountain Chart' where the directions and degrees are indicated. Mountain is just a term for the 24 directions in Feng Shui.

24 Mountain Chart of Feng Shui

General Direction	Exact Direction	Compass Degrees	Energy or Animal
SOUTH	S1	157.6° - 172.5°	Yang Fire
	S2	172.6° - 187.5°	HORSE
	S3	187.6° - 202.5°	Yin Fire
SW	SW1	202.6° - 217.5°	GOAT
	SW2	217.6° - 232.5°	Earth
	SW3	232.6° - 247.5°	MONKEY
WEST	W1	247.6° - 262.5°	Yang Metal
	W2	262.6° - 277.5°	ROOSTER
	W3	277.6° - 292.5°	Yin Metal
NW	NW1	292.6° - 307.5°	DOG
	NW2	307.6° - 322.5°	Metal
	NW3	322.6° - 337.5°	PIG
NORTH	N1	337.6° - 352.5°	Yang Water
	N2	352.6° - 7.5°	RAT
	N3	7.6° - 22.5°	Yin Water
NE	NE1	22.6° - 37.5°	OX
	NE2	37.6° - 52.5°	Earth
	NE3	52.6° - 67.5°	TIGER
EAST	E1	67.6° - 82.5°	Yang Wood
	E2	82.6° - 97.5°	RABBIT
	E3	97.6° - 112.5°	Yin Wood
SE	SE1	112.6° - 127.5°	DRAGON
	SE2	127.6° - 142.5°	Wood
	SE3	142.6° - 157.5°	SNAKE

CHAPTER THREE
The Eight Life-Gua Numbers + Five Elements

In traditional Chinese philosophy and metaphysics, everything in the natural world can be classified into one of five categories of chi or movements of energy, known as *Wu Xing* or the *Five Phases*. As the case with so many brilliant discoveries, nature was the inspiration. The ancients paid close attention to the consistent and predicable cycles of energy—fire burns wood, and metal comes from the earth. By associating this information with the human body and everyday events, the Five Element theory was born. This offered a feasible solution to evaluating the interaction of energy by placing *all* energy into one of the five categories.

These five elements are metal (jin-literally the word for *gold)*, wood (mu), water (shui), fire (ho), and earth (tu). Each element is a representation of matter and energy as it changes from one form to the next. Wu Xing simply illuminates the relationship among these types of energy—and is to be understood as both figurative and literal. It is used extensively in many fields of Eastern thought, such as Feng Shui, Chinese astrology, traditional Chinese medicine, and martial arts. The Five Elements have three cycles; the productive, weakening, and controlling.

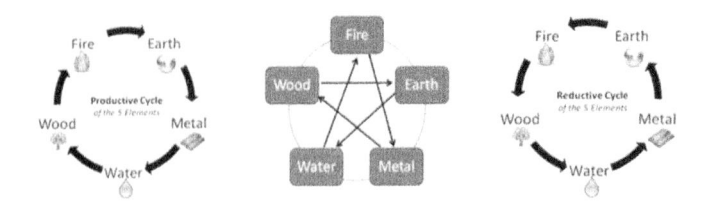

Productive Cycle: Wood feeds fire. Fire produces ash and creates earth. Earth gives birth to metal. Metal melts to a fluid and becomes water, which in turn produces wood.

The Weakening Cycle: This process is the reverse of the productive cycle, because what we give birth to weakens us. Wood stokes fire; therefore, fire weakens wood. Fire generates ash and creates earth; therefore, earth weakens fire. Earth produces metal; therefore, metal weakens earth. Metal melts to a fluid and produces water; therefore, water weakens metal. Water produces wood; therefore, wood weakens water.

The Controlling Cycle: This process is also known as the destructive cycle. Water extinguishes fire, fire melts metal, and metal cuts wood. Wood, in the form of plants or tree roots, controls the earth by breaking it apart or keeping it together. Earth is big enough to hold water—with earth water would have no boundary.

These theories are important when comparing the energies of the Life Guas. For example, we looking at the compatibility of loved ones and partners, it is essential that the elements are in balance and thoroughly analyzed. This offers vital clues on the interaction of family, friends, co-workers and all relationships in our life. For example, a man who is a 1 Life-Gua (water) and his spouse is a 9 Life-Gua (fire), would be an interesting mix. Water puts out fire, but on the positive note, water and fire create steam!

A Review of the Life-Guas Elements
1 Life-Gua (water), 3 and 4 Life Guas (wood), 2 and 8 Life Guas (earth), 6 and 7 life Guas (metal) and the 9 Life-Gua (fire).

The Four 'Perfect' Matches
Eight Mansions have four sets of Life-Guas that are purported to be a perfect match. There's no such thing really, and important to note that other matches can be excellent as well.

East Life Matches:
1 Life-Gua and the 4 Life Gua (water and wood)
3 Life Gua and the 9 Life Gua (wood and fire)

West Life Matches:
2 Life Gua and the 8 Life-Gua (both earth)
6 Life Gua and the 7 Life Gua (both metal)

CHAPTER FOUR
The 12 Chinese Zodiac Animals

The **Chinese Zodiac** is a 12 year cycle. Each year of the 12 year cycle is named after one of the original 12 animals. Each animal has a different personality and different characteristics. The animal is believed to be the main factor in each person's life that gives them their traits, success, and happiness in their lifetime. Scholars say that the Zodiac was brought from India, Hotan, and Sogdiana by the Buddhist people during the Qin dynasty via the famous trade route, Silk Road.

There is a legend or story is that Buddha summoned all of the animals of the earth to come before him before his departure from this earth, but only twelve animals actually came to bid him farewell. To reward the animals who came to him he named a year after each of them, the years were given to them in the order in which they had arrived; it starts with the Rat. The following information will give you the animal year that you were born in. If you were born before February 4th in any give year, use the previous year to get your animal sign. Traditionally, the Chinese masses use the Lunar Calendar to determine their animal Zodiac. However, all Classical Feng Shui systems are based on the Chinese Solar Calendar which begins each year on February 4th as it is very accurate, the Lunar can vary as much as two weeks. You'll have a more accurate picture of your personality when the animal year of your birth is mixed with your personal Life Gua Number.

Each animal is assigned one of the five elements, this is based on the Ganzhi system (stems & branches) and where they are located on the Chinese Luo Pan. The following are the general descriptions of the Animals of the Chinese Zodiac:

YEAR OF THE RAT

Solar Calendar: *Beginning Feb 4th of* **1924, 1936, 1948, 1960, 1972, 1984, 1996, 2008**

Charming, Elegant, Witty

The Rat is yang energy. The first animal in the Zodiac is the witty, imaginative and ever curious rat. Rats are noted for their ability to observe, and therefore they are also able to read people very accurately. Rats are fast and full of energy, talkative, expressive, and charming. They are natural artist and can easily invent things. However, they can become aggressive when provoked. The rat is one of the most enduring of species on the planet, able to survive almost any type of disaster. They move a great deal—homes, jobs, and love to travel. They are loyal in relationships finding it hard to break away and go forward. A good partner needs to be able to keep up with this high-energy personality. **Good Partners and Friends**: Dragon and Monkey **Avoid:** Horse.

YEAR OF THE OX
Beginning Feb 4th of **2009, 1997, 1985, 1973, 1961, 1949, 1937, 1925**

Steadfast, Dependable, Determined

Those born in the year of the Ox are known for their steadfastness, dependability and determination. They possess the ability to work their way to success, and they work hard. The Oxens do not change jobs very often, and are not risk takers. They prefer their own counsel and research over that of others, but they would rather develop life-long relationships to casual one. They are not social creatures, and would rather stay at home. They will take their time finding the perfect partner in life as change is out of the comfort zone for them. **Good Partners and Friends**: Snake and Rooster **Avoid**: Goat.

YEAR OF THE TIGER
Beginning Feb 4th of **2010, 1998, 1986, 1974, 1962, 1950, 1938, 1926**

Intense, Risk-Takers, Spontaneous

Being born under this sign indicates the full force of intense, primal energy that can be over powering for others. Like the powerful cat always aware of his natural environment, they are deeply sensitive. Tiger people have a great deal of influence in any setting, whether it be personal or business and they are natural leaders. They are huge risk-takers, spontaneous, independent and they like to be on top! In relationships they never bore their partners, they are intensely passionate and are born protectors of their mates and children. **Good Partners and Friends:** Horse and Dog. **Avoid:** Monkey.

YEAR OF THE RABBIT
Beginning Feb 4th of **2011, 1999, 1987, 1975, 1963, 1951, 1939, 1927**

Lightening Quick, Sensitive, Stylish

Those born under the sign of the Rabbit are always on the alert and are very sensitive, soft and vulnerable. They are honest, highly intelligent, clever, and their minds move lightening quick. Highly social, they are classy and refined people that are well-mannered and stylish. They tend to be insecure by nature, and do not take risks at all. Rabbits are naturally sensuous and highly sexual. They may have unrealistic expectations and need a partner that will not take advantage of them.
Good Partners and Friends: Goat and Pig. **Avoid:** Rooster

YEAR OF THE DRAGON
Beginning Feb 4th of **2012, 2000, 1988, 1976, 1964, 1952, 1940, 1928**

Powerful, Independent, Hot Tempered

People born under this sign are considered very auspicious as it denotes a great spirit of power. In the Chinese culture the mythical dragon is the mightiest and most revered creatures. These people play by their own rules, and they like things on a grand scale. Even though they may have their head in the clouds with loft ideas, they are grounded. In relationships, they make friends easily and are independent even in romantic ones. Because dragons can have hot tempers, they need a tough-skinned mate, but make loyal life partners.
Good Partners and Friends: Rat and Monkey **Avoid:** Dog

YEAR OF THE SNAKE
Beginning Feb 4th of **2013, 2001, 1989, 1977, 1965, 1953, 1941, 1929**

Patient, Intelligent, Seducers

Those born under the sign of the snake are sensitive, intelligent and are masters at the waiting game. They also know how to get what they want from people, and it is best not to make an enemy of a snake. They are consummate seducers, and in relationships with lovers and partners tend to be possessive and jealous. Their best quality is how they reserve and use their internal energy for powerful results. **Good Partners and Friends:** Ox and Rooster **Avoid:** Pig

YEAR OF THE HORSE
Beginning Feb 4th of **2014, 2002, 1990, 1978, 1966, 1954, 1942, 1930**

Strength, Persistence, Confident

Strength and persistence are the keywords for those born under this sign. They have tremendous inner confidence, love to be the center of attention and are stimulated by the next challenge. Horses are proud and independent but still long for a life partner. They prefer to live in harmony, and with a good mate they can exhibit their full power and spirit. They tend to fall hard and fast in relationships, but get a great deal mellower late in life. **Good Partners and Friends:** Tiger and Dog **Avoid:** Rat

YEAR OF THE GOAT
Beginning Feb 4th of **2015, 2003, 1991, 1979, 1967, 1955, 1943, 1931**

Reliable, Private, Steadfast

Those born under the sign of the Goat are extremely reliable and steadfast; even under undo pressure they remain calm. They have nurturing personalities and are very giving people. They do not enjoy being in the thick of things or the center of attention, instead they like being home alone. Intensely private people, it takes some time and effort to know them. They have a small circle of friends, but will work hard for friends and loved ones. **Good Partners and Friends:** Rabbit and Pig **Avoid:** Ox

YEAR OF THE MONKEY
Beginning Feb 4th of **2016, 2004, 1992, 1980, 1968, 1956, 1944, 1932**

Quick, Intelligent, Promiscuous

Those born under the sign of monkey are quick as lightening! Their minds move at a remarkable speed. They have a talent of learning quickly and their intelligence gives them the ability to hatch new ideas, concepts, and invent new systems. They are playful, and are hard to pin down in relationships, they won't settle quickly. They may even be promiscuous as they are easily bored. However, with an excellent partner, they will commit to that person in every way. **Good Partners and Friends:** Dragon and Rat
Avoid: Tiger

YEAR OF THE ROOSTER
Beginning Feb 4th of **2017, 2005, 1993, 1981, 1969, 1957, 1945, 1933**

Persistent, Honest, Social

People born under this sign have the strength of persistence, and have considerable personal power. They excel in the arts and in human relationships. They tell it like it is, their honesty can sting, and their partner cannot be over sensitive. Roosters are loyal, trustworthy and very social. Those who make the best partners for them will totally get that under their gruffness and sharp opinions beats a heart of gold. **Good Partners and Friends:** Snake and Ox **Avoid:** Rabbit

YEAR OF THE DOG
Beginning Feb 4th of **2018, 2006, 1994, 1982, 1970, 1958, 1946, 1934**

Worrisome, Feeling, Loyal

Those born under the sign of dog are loyal and ready for action; they often offer kind words and useful advice. They have a good ear for listening. Whatever they focus and turn their attention to, they will develop competence. They will always find a way to complete an assignment. These people are graced with good fortune and deep feelings. In relationships they have trouble trusting others, and are often scared off by the dog's insecure, worrisome and anxious nature. **Good Partners and Friends**: Horse and Tiger **Avoid:** Dragon

YEAR OF THE PIG
Beginning Feb 4th of **2019, 2007, 1995, 1983, 1971, 1959, 1947, 1935**

Generous, Accumulators, Affectionate

Those born under the sign of the Pig can exhibit generosity, diligence and compassion. The pot belly of the pig makes them great accumulators—wealth, energy, or wisdom. Pigs are highly intelligent and very perceptive people. They are affectionate, highly sexual and make great partner. Pigs can posses an inner power that makes them reliable and wise in the times of a great crisis. **Good Partners and Friends:** Goat and Rabbits **Avoid:** Snake

Keep in mind that rarely is it possible to get the most perfect match in energy with Life Guas and the animal year of birth. However, some seem to naturally clash according to Feng Shui.

The Twelve Animals	
Animal	**Element**
RAT	water
Ox	earth
Tiger	wood
RABBIT	wood
Dragon	earth
Snake	fire
HORSE	fire
Goat	earth
Monkey	metal
ROOSTER	metal
Dog	earth
Pig	water

The Six Clashes

Here are the famous, six 'clashes'; these relationships can be difficult and are known as the six sets of incompatibilities between the Chinese Zodiac signs.

Rat ⟷ Horse
Ox ⟷ Goat
Tiger ⟷ Monkey
Rabbit ⟷ Rooster
Dragon ⟷ Dog
Snake ⟷ Pig

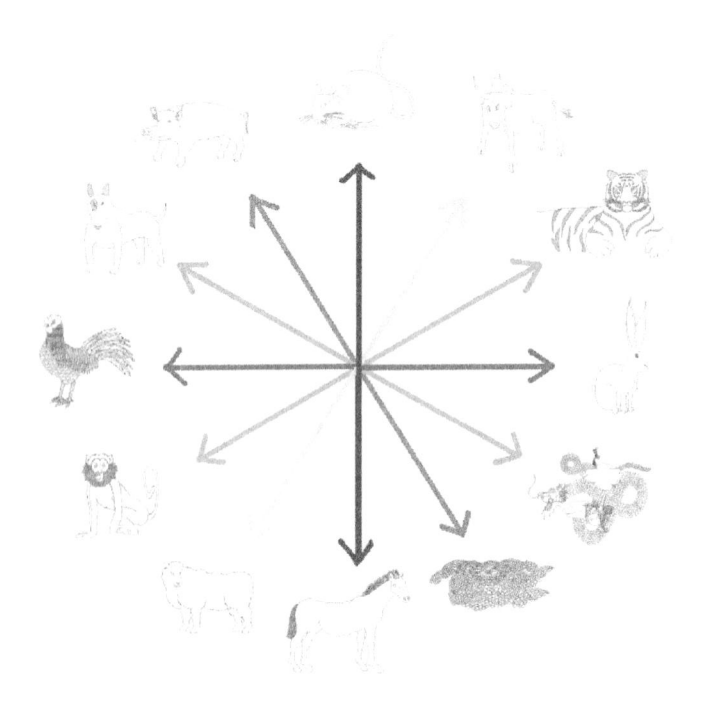

The Four Trines

This information is very useful in seeing the luck of a person in any given year. It also is used to examine world events and the elemental energies. These *groups* are also very compatible as well.

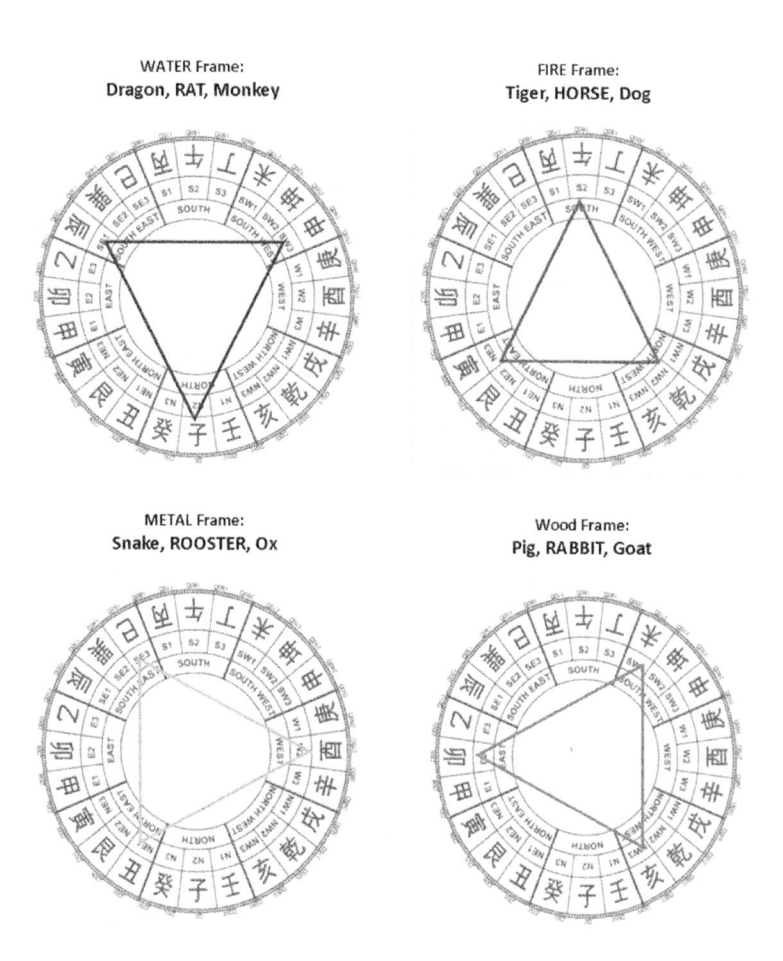

WATER Frame:
Dragon, RAT, Monkey

FIRE Frame:
Tiger, HORSE, Dog

METAL Frame:
Snake, ROOSTER, Ox

Wood Frame:
Pig, RABBIT, Goat

The Animal 'Hours'

The animals are also used to mark the hours of the day. However, the Chinese use two-hour increments to do so. The animal hours offer yet another perspective and subtle nuance to detect personality traits for the hour of birth. For instance, the Rat is more alert at night while it is the opposite for the Ox who works hard during the day and sleeps at night. The Tiger will hunt and prowl at night. The Rabbit is cautious in the early morning hours. The Dragon is in 'power' in the early morning hours. The Snake is it's element in the evening hours of love and leisure. The Horse is a daytime animal while the Goat is best in early evening. The Monkey is cunning in the afternoon. The Rooster is best and crows in early morning hours. The Dog shines with its loyalty in the early evening while the Pig just goes to sleep.

Twelve Animal Hours	
Animal	Hour
RAT	11:00 PM to 1:00 AM
Ox	1:00 AM to 3:00 AM
Tiger	3:00 AM to 5:00 AM
RABBIT	5:00 AM to 7:00 AM
Dragon	7:00 AM to 9:00 AM
Snake	9:00 AM to 11:00 AM
HORSE	11:00 AM to 1:00 PM
Goat	1:00 PM to 3:00 PM
Monkey	3:00 PM to 5:00 PM
ROOSTER	5:00 PM to 7:00 PM
Dog	7:00 PM to 9:00 PM
Pig	9:00 PM to 11:00 PM

CHAPTER FIVE
Life-Gua Zodiac Personalities

The Life-Guas matched up with the Animal Year of Birth gives specific details into a person's career choices, romance or martial partners, possible health issues and more. For example, a 1-Gua born in the *Year of the Pig* is quite different than a 1-Gua born in the *Year of the Horse*.

In this chapter we will fully explore several important and key aspects of Eight Mansions involving the eight Life-Guas (some masters call this the *Ming Gua*). In arriving at your personal Life Gua Number, you have information on which directions support you and those that can bring trouble. Also, based on your Life Gua, you're assigned certain personality traits, energy and characteristics. Do keep in mind that they are general and not meant to be the definitive; however I find after consulting with thousands of clients, that they are very accurate.

The personality narratives work very similar to astrology; each Life Gua will have an element (water, wood, fire, earth or metal) and this energy will influence the person's behavior, habits, physical looks, health issues, attraction to specific occupations, thinking process, and sexual desires; both negative and positive in all these areas. I call these portrayals the **Life Gua Personalities™**.

Even though the Life-Gua gives great insights into our personalities (and the 4 categories), I noticed that not all Life Guas were created equal. While in general, for example, the 1 Life Guas are very intelligent, secretive, love freedom and are highly sensuous, they can be very different depending on the animal year in which they were born. For example a 1 Gua born in the *Year of the Snake* is very different than the 1 Gua born in the *Year of the Horse*. So, I decided to once again expand the Life Gua Personalities by matching them with the animal year of birth; this gave a more specific picture of the personality traits.

On the next several pages you will find all eight Life Guas combined with the 12 Chinese Zodiac Animal signs; there are 96 possible combinations, however some Life Guas never match up with certain animal years. For example, those born in either the Year of the Ox, Dragon, Goat or Dog will only be a 3, 6, or 9 Gua. Other combinations will be exclusive for either men or women.

Year of the
Rat

1 Gua as a Rat
MEN ONLY!
Sensuous ● *High Strung* ● *Survivors*
Elements: Yang **Water** and Yang **Water**

Year begins Feb 4th
Years occurring for Males: **1936, 1972, 2008, 2044**
Note: No female 1 Guas are ever born in the Year of the Rat

Famous 1 Gua-Rat Men: Vidal Sassoon, Buddy Holly, Engelbert Humperdinck, Glen Campbell, Kris Kristofferson, Albert Finney, Wilt Chamberlain, Robert Redford, Burt Reynolds, Bobby Darin, Jim Henson, Bruce Dern, Yves Saint-Laurent, Louis Gossett Jr., Jude Law, Marlon Wayans, Eminem, Dane Cook, Josh Duhamel, Antonio Sabato Jr., and Marlon Wayans.

Personality & Romance: The 1 Gua men who are born in the *Year of the Rat* is a double water sign making them extremely emotional, sensuous, and high strung. These men are highly intelligent, imaginative, and very charming. The water-water combination also enhances their natural intuitive abilities in sizing people up; when provoked the 1 Gua-Rat can become very aggressive. With the appearance of a cool and dignified exterior, deep down these men tend to be insecure and react very well to praise rather than being criticized. As one of the oldest survivors on the planet, their energy adapts, endures and overcomes almost any challenge presented.

They love being free, mobile and the excitement of travel. The 1 Gua-Rats tend to be very loyal in relationships; they need a partner who can handle their deep sexuality, moodiness, high energy and intenseness. If they have love affairs, they are still loyal to their wives and family—these temptations are never *loves of the heart*, just dalliances.

The best stuff: When the 1 Gua-Rats are fully exhibiting their best qualities, they are very intelligent, forthright, disciplined, systematic, meticulous, charismatic, charming, cool and dignified, hardworking, industrious, charming, eloquent, sociable and shrewd. *The worst stuff:* When the 1 Gua-Rats move to the darker side of their nature, they can be manipulative, cruel, dictatorial, rigid, selfish, obstinate, critical, over-ambitious, ruthless, intolerant, scheming, and sturdy.

Career: Some of the best professions for the 1 Gua-Rats, where they may attain wealth, fame or fulfillment, are as/in writers, broadcasters, actors, advisors, counselors, lawyers, politicians, designers, engineers, managers, directors, administrators, entrepreneurs, musicians, stand-up comedians, researchers, historians, race car drivers, sales, finance, banking, freight, shipping, spa, communications, entertainment, pub/bar, ice freezing, tourism, fishing, firefighting, water produce, police, sex industry, diplomat, artist, painter, or in the publishing industry.

2 Gua as a Rat
WOMEN ONLY!
Calm ● *Intelligent* ● *Intuitive*
Elements: Yin **Earth** and Yang **Water**

Year begins Feb 4th
Years occurring for Females: **1924, 1960, 1996, 2032**
Note: No male 2 Guas are ever born in the Year of the Rat

Famous 2 Gua-Rat Women: Ruby Dee, Eva Marie Saint, Kelly LeBrock, Dorothy Stratten, Carol Alt, Emma Samms, Roma Downey, Meg Tilly, Robin Roberts, Jennifer Grey, Kristin Scott Thomas, Sarah Brightman, Daryl Hannah, Julianne Moore, Valerie Bertinelli, Carol Alt, Greta Scacchi, and Amy Grant.

Personality & Romance: The 2 Gua born in the *Year of the Rat* is a mix of earth and water energy bringing a bit more emotion to their normal, calm-nature. The 2 Gua-Rats are very intuitive, observing people with sharp accuracy. These women are attracted to the healing arts such as Psychiatry in which they can use their energy and communicative skills. They make talented doctors with a compassionate, charming 'bedside' manner that is reassuring to those in their care. The 2 Gua Rats are survivors, comfortable in dark spaces and have relaxed demeanors but can be rigid as well. Since their energy is very yin, if not kept in check, the 2 Gua Rats can suffer from depression. Focusing on their creative side and love of travel will keep their energy high and expressed in productive outlets. *The best stuff:* When the 2 Gua-Rats are fully exhibiting their best qualities, they are forthright, disciplined, systematic, meticulous, charismatic, hardworking, industrious, charming, eloquent, sociable, and shrewd. *The worst stuff:* When the 2 Gua-Rats move to the darker side of their nature, they can be manipulative, cruel, dictatorial, rigid, selfish, obstinate, critical, depressed, over-ambitious, ruthless, intolerant, scheming, and sturdy.

Career: Some of the best professions for the 2 Gua-Rats, where they may attain wealth, fame or fulfillment, are as/in writers, broadcasters, actors, advisors, counselors, lawyers, politicians, designers, engineers, managers, directors, administrators, entrepreneurs, musicians, stand-up comedians, researchers, historians, race car drivers, sales, accounting, retail, publishing, musician, instructor, property, real estate, construction, earthenware, consultancy, hotel, insurance, architecture, and interior design.

4 Gua as a Rat
MEN ONLY!
Gentle ● *Charming* ● *Witty*
Elements: Yin **Wood** and Yang **Water**

Year begins Feb 4th
Years occurring for Males: **1924, 1960, 1996, 2032**
Note: No female 4 Guas are ever born in the Year of the Rat

Famous 4 Gua-Rat Men: Dale Carnegie, Harpo Marx, Ed Koch, Marlon Brando, Marcello Mastroianni, Henry Mancini, Sean Penn, David Duchovny, John Kennedy Jr., Hugh Grant, Antonio Banderas, Jean-Claude Van Damme, Colin Firth, RuPaul, James Spader, Prince Andrew, Stanley Tucci, Kenneth Branagh, and Stefano Casiraghi.

Personality & Romance: The 4 Gua men born in the *Year of the Rat* are a harmonious mix of wood and water energy; this creates sharp minded wit and irresistible charm! To the world, they have a cool & dignified persona, but deep down they are insecure. The 4 Gua-Rats thrive on praise, recognition and popularity. They resent being ordered around or made to feel small. If they are corned or feel trapped, they can become aggressive, stay on their good side as their true nature is gentle. These men have very progressive energy and ideas; they often become famous in the writing, acting or as an entrepreneur. In dealing with these men, you must use diplomacy as they can be overly sensitive to any type of criticism.

They are loyal in relationships finding it hard to break away and go forward. A good partner needs to be able to keep up with this high-energy personality. When the 4 Gua-Rats step into their negative side, they can be obstinate, ruthless, rigid and selfish. However, they are genuinely romantic and sentimental in relationships.

The best stuff: When the 4 Gua-Rats are fully exhibiting their best qualities, they are forthright, disciplined, systematic, meticulous, gentle, charismatic, hardworking, industrious, charming, eloquent, sociable and shrewd. *The worst stuff:* When the 4 Gua-Rats move to the darker side of their nature, they can be indecisive, manipulative, cruel, dictatorial, rigid, selfish, obstinate, critical, over-ambitious, wishy-washy, ruthless, intolerant and scheming.

Career: Some of the best professions for the 4 Gua-Rats, where they may attain wealth, fame or fulfillment, are as/in Writers, Broadcasters, Actors, Advisors, Counselors, Lawyers, Politicians, Designers, Engineers, Managers, Directors, Administrators, Entrepreneurs, Musicians, Stand-up Comedians, Researchers, Historians, Race Car Drivers, Finances, Publishing, , Musicians, Law, the Arts, Entrepreneurs, Actors, Counselors, Campaigners, Education, Social Services, Medicine, Pharmaceuticals, Print media, Bookstores, Farming, Agriculture, Textiles, Fashion, Technicians,

7 Gua as a Rat
MEN ONLY!
Talkative ● *Sexual* ● *Charming*
Elements: Yin **Metal** and Yang **Water**

Year begins Feb 4th
Years occurring for Males: **1912, 1948, 1984, 2020**
Note: No male 7 Guas are ever born in the Year of the Rat

Famous 7 Gua-Rat Men: Gene Kelly, Perry Como, Karl Malden, Art Linkletter, James Taylor, Cat Stevens, Terry Bradshaw, Mikhail Baryshnikov, Gérard Depardieu, Jeremy Irons, Andrew Lloyd Webber, Richard Simmons, Jean Reno, Trey Songz, and Fernando Torres.

Personality & Romance: The 7 Guas born in the *Year of the Rat* are a harmonious mix of metal and water energy; these men are charming, confident, witty, insecure, talkative, and have engaging personalities. They are usually very interesting men and make great partners and lovers. The 7 Gua Rats tend to be restless, impulsive and need a great deal of praise and flattery; be cognizant of not injuring their sensitive egos with direct or, even implied criticism. While these men are not great risk-takers, they make inventive entrepreneurs, good negotiators, and clever tacticians. The 7 Gua-Rats love the pleasures of life such as good food, good sex, good conversation, and so forth. They can be fully charged at the beginning of a relationship, romantic and sentimental; they love to take care of their partners. These men take marriage very seriously and are faithful in romantic relationships. They can be charismatic, smooth-talking, or have a razor-sharp tongue—especially if backed into a corner where they may also become aggressive. When the 7 Gua-Rats move to the dark side of their nature they can be critical, ruthless, intolerant, obstinate and dictatorial.

The best stuff: When the 7 Gua-Rats are fully exhibiting their best qualities, they are forthright, disciplined, systematic, meticulous, charismatic, hardworking, industrious, charming, eloquent, sociable and shrewd. *The worst stuff:* When the 7 Gua-Rats move to the darker side of their nature, they can be manipulative, cruel, dictatorial, rigid, selfish, obstinate, critical, over-ambitious, ruthless, intolerant, scheming, and sturdy.

Career: Some of the best professions for the 7 Gua-Rats, where they may attain wealth, fame or fulfillment, are as/in Writers, Broadcasters, Actors, Advisors, Counselors, Lawyers, Politicians, Designers, Engineers, Managers, Directors, Administrators, Entrepreneurs, Musicians, Stand-up Comedians, Researchers, Historians, Race Car Drivers, Farming, Estate Management, Medicine, Philosopher, Teacher, Chef, Police Office, Engineering, IT, Computers, Goldsmith, Hardware, Machinery, Metal Mining, Excavation, Hi-tech Goods, Internet, Lawyer, Judging, White Goods, Metal Jewelry, Government service, Sports Equipment and Lecturers.

8 Gua as a Rat
WOMEN ONLY!
Witty ● *Sexual* ● *Magnetic*
Elements: Yang **Earth** and Yang **Water**

Year begins Feb 4th
Years occurring for Females: **1912, 1936, 1948, 1984, 2008, 2020, 2044**
Note: No female 8 Guas are ever born in the Year of the Rat

Famous 8 Gua-Rat Women: Eva Braun, Sonja Henie, Julia Child, Doris Duke, Ursula Andress, Mary Tyler Moore, Ruth Buzzi, , Stevie Nicks, Grace Jones, Barbara Hershey, Margot Kidder, Kathy Bates, Barbara Mandrell, JoBeth Williams, Tina Sinatra, , Cheryl Burke, and Ashlee Simpson.

Personality & Romance: The 8 Gua women born in the *Year of the Rat* is a combination of earth and water energy; this will cause some emotional tension. These women are steadfast, witty, magnetic, hardworking, vivacious and dynamic. While the 8 Gua-Rats may resist change, they can deftly handle trouble without falling apart. They tend to be a bit old-fashioned in relationships wanting marriage and babies above a career. They fear being alone and must always have a man in their life; even when life is bringing them success and independence, she will give it up to have a spouse and security. These women are full of energy, talkative, expressive, and charming; however they can become aggressive when provoked. They are talented with things of the earth-construction, real estate, and landscaping. They move a great deal—homes, jobs, and love to travel. They are loyal in relationships finding it hard to break away and go forward. A good partner needs to be able to keep up with this high-energy personality. When they exhibit the dark side of their nature, they can be hoarders, dictatorial, rigid, selfish, obstinate, critical, over-ambitious, ruthless, and intolerant.

The best stuff: When the 8 Gua-Rats are fully exhibiting their best qualities, they are forthright, disciplined, systematic, meticulous, charismatic, hardworking, industrious, charming, eloquent, sociable, noble and shrewd. *The worst stuff:* When the 8 Gua-Rats move to the darker side of their nature, they can be manipulative, cruel, dictatorial, rigid, selfish, obstinate, critical, stubborn, over-ambitious, ruthless, intolerant, scheming, and sturdy.

Career: Some of the best professions for the 8 Gua-Rats, where they may attain wealth, fame or fulfillment, are as Writers, Broadcasters, Actors, Advisors, Counselors, Lawyers, Politicians, Designers, Engineers, Managers, Directors, Administrators, Entrepreneurs, Musicians, Stand-up Comedians, Researchers, Historians, Race Car Drivers, Publishing, Finance, Music, Property, Real Estate, Construction, Earthenware, Consultancy, Hotel, Insurance, Architecture, Pottery, Recruitment, Quarry, Human Resources, Farmers, OB-GYN, and Nuns.

Year of the Ox

3 Gua as an Ox
FOR MEN & WOMEN!
Enterprising ● *Steady* ● *Outspoken*
Elements: Yang **Wood** and Yin **Earth**

Year begins Feb 4th
Years occurring for Males & Females:
1925, 1961, 1997, 2033

Famous 3 Gua-Oxen Men & Women: Rock Hudson, Tony Curtis, Angela Lansbury, Robert F. Kennedy, Princess Diana, Melissa Etheridge, Eddie Murphy, Enya, Nadia Comaneci, Mariel Hemingway, Laurence Fishburne, k.d. lang, Heather Locklear, Dennis Rodman, Bonnie Hunt, and Jeremy Northam.

Personality & Romance: The 3 Guas born in the *Year of the Ox* are a mix of wood and earth energy causing a bit of inner turmoil; with the right outlet however, it is mitigated. With a dependable and steady nature, these men and women work hard with a methodical, focused determination. The 3 Gua-Oxens prefer to develop life-long relationships to casual ones. They will take their time finding the perfect partner in life as change is out of the comfort zone for them. These Guas are full of energy that is often punctuated with bursts of nervousness. Tending towards outspokenness, they often surprise or shock those around them. Because the 3 Gua-Oxens are prone to spreading their energy a little thin, committing to too much, they are often fall into overwhelm. When they move to the darker side of their nature, they can become demanding and rigid.

The best stuff: When the 3 Gua-Oxens are fully exhibiting their best qualities, they are dependable, calm, methodical, patient, organized, hardworking, ambitious, conventional, steady, modest, logical, resolute, and tenacious. *The worst stuff:* When the 3 Gua-Oxens move to the darker side of their nature, they can be outspoken, stubborn, narrow-minded, brash, materialistic, nervous, rigid, demanding.

Career: Some of the best professions for the 3 Gua-Oxens, where they may attain wealth, fame or fulfillment, are in agriculture, manufacturing, pharmacy, mechanics, engineering, draftsmanship, artistry, politics, real estate, interior design, painting, carpentry, quarry work, Estate Management, Farming, Philosophy, Entertainers, Chef, Police Officer, Education, Social Services, Medicine, Pharmaceuticals, Print media, Publishing, Bookstores, Farming, Agriculture, Textiles, Fashion, Technicians, Musicians, Broadcast Announcers, and Transportation.

6 Gua as an Ox
MEN & WOMEN!
Ambitious ● *Authoritative* ● *Methodical*
Elements: Yang **Metal** and Yin **Earth**

Year begins Feb 4th
Years occurring for Males**: 1913, 1949, 1985, 2009, 2021.** Years occurring for Females: **1901, 1937, 1973, 2045**

Famous 6 Gua-Ox Men & Women: Burt Lancaster, Red Skelton, Gerald R. Ford, Lionel Richie, Richard Gere, Billy Joel, Bruce Springsteen, Bruce Jenner, David Foster, Tom Berenger, Jeff Bridges, Rick Springfield, Aishwarya Rai Bachchan, Monica Lewinsky, Kate Beckinsale, Heidi Klum, Tori Spelling, Molly Sims Kristen Wiig, Derek Hough, Kris Humphries, Bruno Mars, Cristiano Ronaldo, T-Pain and Michael Phelps.

Personality & Romance: The 6 Guas born in the *Year of the Ox* are a harmonious mix of metal and earth energy; this makes these men and women steadfast, dependable and methodical. The 6 Gua-Oxens are not particularly romantic; however they can be very passionate and extraordinarily loyal to their partners. These men and women are highly principled and disciplined mixed with steely determination. Neither sex is showy; preferring to develop the intellect than to dress to 'strut you stuff' or as a seductress.

The 6 Gua-Oxens do not like excess, frivolity and flaunting their wealth. The men can be ruthless, tough and the women judgmental as they cannot tolerate idle gossip or silly behavior; they are not naturally social preferring to stay at home. They feel comfortable with positions of power and authority, making righteous leaders. When these men and women move into the negative side of their personalities they can be stubborn, narrow-minded, rigid and demanding.

The best stuff: When the 6 Gua-Oxens are fully exhibiting their best qualities, they are dependable, calm, methodical, patient, hardworking, ambitious, conventional, steady, modest, logical, resolute and tenacious. *The worst stuff:* When the 6 Gua-Oxens move to the darker side of their nature, they can be stubborn, narrow-minded, judgmental, materialistic, rigid and demanding.

Career: Some of the best professions for the 6 Gua-Oxens, where they may attain wealth, fame or fulfillment, are in agriculture, manufacturing, pharmacy, mechanics, engineering, draftsmanship, artistry, politics, real estate, interior design, painting, carpentry, quarry work, Farming, Estate Management, Medicine, Philosopher, Teacher, Chef, Police Office Engineering, IT, Computers, Goldsmith, Hardware, Machinery, Metal Mining, Excavation, Hi-tech Goods, Internet, Lawyer, Judging, White Goods, Metal Jewelry, Government service, Sports Equipment, Clocks, Lecturers.

9 Gua as an Ox
MEN & WOMEN!
Confident ● *Brilliant* ● *Loyal*
Elements: Yin **Fire** and Yin **Earth**

Year begins Feb 4th
Years occurring for Males: **1901, 1937, 1973, 2009, 2045.** Years occurring for Females: **1913, 1949, 1985, 2021**

Famous 9 Gua Oxen Men & Women: Rosa Parks, Vivien Leigh, , Morgan Freeman, Anthony Hopkins, Dustin Hoffman, George Carlin, Ridley Scott, Joyce DeWitt, Shelley Long, Twiggy, Sigourney Weaver, Ivana Trump, Vera Wang, Leslie Van Houten, Yasmin Khan, Annie Leibovitz, Paul Walker, Akon, Adrien Brody, Nick Lachey, Peter Facinelli, Neil Patrick Harris, Peter Andre, Ashley Tisdale, Bar Refaeli, Ciara, Amanda Seyfried, Keira Knightley, and Carey Mulligan.

Personality & Romance: The 9 Gua men & women who were born in the *Year of the Ox* are an auspicious mix of fire and earth energy; this creates inner confidence and stability. These men and women are honest, patriotic, ambitious, family-oriented, free-spirited and highly intelligent. They are famously diligent, determined and hard-working. The 9 Gua-Oxens are not influenced by others and do things according to their own ideas and abilities; before taking action to do anything, they will have a specific plan and detailed steps, add to this their physical strength and these people will enjoy great success. The 9 Gua-Oxens have a sharp, brilliant intellect; they can also be wise, loyal, and sentimental. Blessed with a fiery spirit and energy, these people have a decided adventurous streak. They are not particularly romantic; rather will take a more practical approach to selecting a spouse. They prefer their own counsel over that of others, and would rather develop life-long relationships to casual ones. With concentrated and focused effort, they can reach great height of achievements and standing in the world.

The best stuff: When the 9 Gua-Oxens are fully exhibiting their best qualities, they are radiant, steadfast, loyal, social, methodical, patient, hardworking, ambitious, conventional, steady, modest, logical, resolute, and tenacious. *The worst stuff:* When the 9 Gua-Oxens move to the darker side of their nature, they can be paranoid, unforgiving, ruthless, domineering, psychotic, unstable, stubborn, narrow-minded, materialistic, rigid, demanding.

Career: Some of the best professions for the 9 Gua-Oxens, where they may attain wealth, fame or fulfillment, are in medicine, religion, teaching, philosophy, agriculture, manufacturing, pharmacy, mechanics, engineering, draftsmanship, artistry, politics, real estate, interior design, painting, carpentry, or quarry work, Acting, Show business, Public speaking, Fuel/Oil, Chemicals, Optical, Cosmetics, Advertising, Television, Restaurants, Lighting, Beauty, Writers, War Correspondence, and Soldiers.

Year of the
Tiger

The 1 Gua as a Tiger
WOMEN ONLY!
Leaders ● *Risk-Takers* ● *Raw Energy*
Elements: Yang **Water** and Yang **Wood**
Year begins Feb 4th
Years occurring for Females: **1914, 1950, 1986, 2022**

Note: No male 1 Guas are ever born in the Year of the Tiger

Famous 1 Gua-Tiger Women: Dorothy Lamou, Karen Carpenter, Cybill Shepherd, Natalie Cole, Joan Lunden, Susan Anton, Arianna Huffington, Deniece Williams, Cristina Ferrare, Patti Austin, Christina Onassis, Dianna Agron, Leighton Meester, Camilla Belle, Amber Heard, Lea Michele, Ellie Goulding, Megan Fox, Amanda Bynes, and Mary-Kate & Ashley Olsen.

Personality & Romance: The 1 Gua born in the *Year of the Tiger* is a mix of water and wood elements, making their energy progressive, powerful, commanding and usually the 'smartest person in the room'. These women are gutsy and are natural leaders due to their highly developed intelligence. They exhibit and have a natural, primal and raw energy that is almost palatable. The 1 Gua-Tigers are huge risk-takers, spontaneous using their charm and independent nature to influence people in any setting to always come out on top. Despite their powerful energy, they can be very vulnerable, and often become victims of their own outrageous, unchecked passions. They can get bored with their partners quite easily and may move from lover to lover—all in the pursuit of finding true love. In general, they are very talented at making money; they also may squander it. In relationships, the 1 Gua-Tiger women never bore their partners; they are intensely passionate and are protective of their mates, employees, children and anyone under their care.

The best stuff: When the 1 Gua-Tigers are fully exhibiting their best qualities, they are powerful, passionate, daring, stimulating, sincere, affectionate, humanitarian and generous. *The worst stuff:* When the 1 Gua-Tigers move to the darker side of their nature, they can be restless, reckless, impatient, secretive, quick-tempered, moody, obstinate, and selfish.

Career: Some of the best professions for the 1 Gua-Tigers, where they may attain wealth, fame or fulfillment, as/are in Advertising Agent, Office Manager, Actor, Writer, Artist, Airline Pilot, Flight Attendant, Musician, Comedian, Travel, Design, Politics, Police Officer, Travel Writer, Military, Explorer, Advertising, Business Executive, Sales, finance, banking, freight, shipping, spa, communications, entertainment, pub/bar, ice freezing, tourism, fishing, firefighting, water produce, police, sex Industry, diplomat, artist, painter, or in the publishing industry.

2 Gua as a Tiger
MEN ONLY!
Primal Energy ● *Protective* ● *Passionate*
Elements: Yin **Earth** and Yang **Wood**

Year begins Feb 4th
Years occurring for Males: **1914, 1926, 1950, 1962, 1986, 1998, 2022, 2034**

Note: No female 2 Guas are ever born in the Year of the Tiger

Famous 2 Gua-Tiger Men: Joe DiMaggio, Jack LaLanne, Andy Griffith, Chuck Berry, Tony Bennett, David Cassidy, Stevie Wonder, Huey Lewis, Bruce Boxleitner, Gabriel Byrne, Peter Frampton, William Hurt, Jay Leno, Ed Harris, Teddy Pendergrass, Bill Murray, Dr. Phil McGraw, Axl Rose, William H. Macy, Tommy Lee, Ralph Fiennes, Garth Brooks, M.C. Hammer, Clint Black, Usain Bolt, Shia LaBeouf and Robert Pattinson.

Personality & Romance: The 2 Gua-Tiger is a mix of earth and wood energy making them intense, but with a calm, self-assured and primal energy. Like the powerful cat always aware of his natural environment, they are deeply sensitive & intuitive. They have a great deal of influence in any setting—personal or business—and they are natural, instinctive leaders. The 2 Gua-Tigers are men that are huge risk-takers, spontaneous, independent and they thrive by being on top! As they tend to be very passionate in relationships, they never bore their partners. Their natural, nurturing energy makes them very protective of what 'belongs' to them.

The best stuff: When the 2 Gua-Tigers are fully exhibiting their best qualities, they are nurturing, unpredictable, colorful, powerful, passionate, daring, vigorous, stimulating, sincere, affectionate, humanitarian, and generous. *The worst stuff:* When the 2 Gua-Tigers move to the darker side of their nature, they can be rebellious, impulsive, restless, reckless, impatient, quick-tempered, obstinate, and selfish.

Career: Some of the best professions for the **2 Gua-Tigers, where they may attain wealth, fame or fulfillment,** as/are in Advertising Agent, Office Manager, Actor, Writer, Artist, Airline Pilot, Flight Attendant, Musician, Comedian, Travel, Design, Politics, Military, Police Officer, Travel Writer, Explorer, Advertising, Business Executive, Property, Real Estate, Construction, Earthenware, Consultancy, Hotel, Insurance, Architecture, Interior Design, Pottery, Recruitment, Quarry, Human Resources, Handyman, Farmer, OB-GYN, Monks, & Clergyman.

4 Gua as a Tiger
WOMEN ONLY!
Intense ● *Protective* ● *Sex-Appeal*
Elements: Yin **Wood** and Yang **Wood**

Year begins Feb 4th
Years occurring for Females: **1926, 1962, 1998, 2034**
Note: No male 4 Guas are ever born in the Year of the Tiger

Famous 4 Gua-Tiger Women: Marilyn Monroe, Jodie Foster, Sheryl Crow, Paula Abdul, Felicity Huffman, Taylor Dayne, Star Jones, Genie Francis, Kristy McNichol, Gina Gershon, and Laura San Giacomo.

Personality & Romance: The 4 Guas born in the *Year of the Tiger* is pure wood energy making these women extremely progressive and exciting with lots of potent sex-appeal! Old-fashioned Chinese parents do not like their sons marrying Tiger women believing it ill-fated as these ladies have such intense, indecisive and flamboyant energy.

While it is true that the 4 Gua Tigers are all about passion and excitement, they are very protective of those who are lucky enough to win their heart. So fiercely passionate, these ladies tend to be their own worst enemy with their do or die approach to life and relationships. While they are easily influenced, often blowing with the wind, the 4 Gua-Tiger women can still make very devoted, protective and responsible mothers and wives. These ladies are huge risk-takers, spontaneous, direct & honest, and independent—they love being on top. When they move into the negative aspects of their personality they are rebellious, reckless, selfish and impatient.

The best stuff: When the 4 Gua-Tigers are fully exhibiting their best qualities, they are unpredictable, rebellious, colorful, powerful, passionate, daring, impulsive, vigorous, stimulating, sincere, affectionate, humanitarian and generous. *The worst stuff:* When the 4 Gua-Tigers move to the darker side of their nature, they can be restless, reckless, impatient, quick-tempered, indecisive, obstinate, and selfish.

Career: Some of the best professions for the 4 Gua-Tigers, where they may attain wealth, fame or fulfillment, as/are in Advertising Agent, Office Manager, Actor, Writer, Artist, Airline Pilot, Flight Attendant, Musician, Comedian, Travel, Design Politics, Police Officer, Explorer, Advertising, Executives, Law, the Arts, Entrepreneurs, Actors, Counselors, Campaigners, Education, Social Services, Medicine, Pharmaceuticals, Print media, Publishing, Bookstores, Farming, Agriculture, Textiles, Fashion, Technicians, Musicians, and Broadcasting.

7 Gua as a Tiger
WOMEN ONLY!
Impulsive ● *Sexy* ● *Passionate*
Elements: Yin **Metal** and Yang **Wood**

Year begins Feb 4th
Years occurring for Females: **1902, 1938, 1974, 2010, 2046**

Note: No male 7 Guas are ever born in the Year of the Tiger

Famous 7 Gua-Tiger Women: Natalie Wood, Claudia Cardinale, Diana Rigg, Connie Stevens, Eva Mendes, Victoria Beckham, Penélope Cruz, Kate Moss, Jenna Jameson, Jillian Michaels, Hilary Swank, Kimberly 'Lil' Kim' Jones, Amy Fisher, Alanis Morissette, Elizabeth Banks, and Victoria Silvstedt.

Personality & Romance: The 7 Gua women born in the *Year of the Tiger* is an inauspicious mix of metal and wood energy; causing inner turbulence and unrest. These women are passionate, impulsive, protective, enthusiastic, and excessive with exciting, powerful sexual allure! The 7 Gua-Tigers tackle things with enthusiasm, optimism and determination that ensure their success in work or projects. They make talented and efficient leaders and are the most loyal and generous of friends. They are huge risk-takers, spontaneous, independent and they like to be on top! In the areas of love and romance, these women often get carried away with their passions, making them victims of love gone bad; at times they can fall into the charms of manipulative and immoral men. The 7 Gua-Tigers may tend towards the 'excessive' and extremes—too much sex, too much food, too many radical ideas or opinions and so forth. They may have many lovers as they get bored very easily especially if the heartthrob of the moment turns out to be predictable. In the end, they long for a mate that is constant, steady and allows the natural instincts of a tigress to blossom—protective mothers and loyal, passionate wives. When the 7 Gua-Tigers exhibit the negative side of their personality they can be restless, reckless, impatient, quick-tempered, obstinate, and selfish.

The best stuff: When the 7 Gua-Tigers are fully exhibiting their best qualities, they are unpredictable, rebellious, colorful, powerful, passionate, daring, impulsive, vigorous, stimulating, sincere, affectionate, humanitarian and generous. *The worst stuff:* When the 7 Gua-Tigers move to the darker side of their nature, they can be restless, reckless, impatient, quick-tempered, obstinate and selfish.

Career: Some of the best professions for the 7 Gua-Tigers, where they may attain wealth, fame or fulfillment, are in advertising, office management, travel agent, actor, writer, artist, pilot, flight attendant, musician, comedian, chauffeur, Farming, Estate Management, Medicine, Philosopher, Teacher, Chef, Police Office Engineering, IT, Computers, Goldsmith, Hardware, Machinery, Metal Mining, Excavation, Hi-tech Goods, Internet, Lawyer, Judging, White Goods, Metal Jewelry, Government service, Sports Equipment and Lecturers.

8 Gua as a Tiger
MEN ONLY!
Risk-takers ● *Dazzling* ● *Independent*
Elements: Yang **Earth** and Yang **Wood**

Year begins Feb 4th
Years occurring for Males: **1938, 1974, 2010, 2046**
Note: No female 8 Guas are ever born in the Year of the Tiger

Famous 8 Gua Tiger Men: John Steinbeck, Bobby Jones, Oliver Reed, Karl Lagerfeld, Bill Withers, Peter Jennings, Elliott Gould, Joaquin Phoenix, Ryan Seacrest, Ryan Phillippe, Jimmy Fallon, and CeeLo Green.

Personality & Romance: The 8 Gua men born in the *Year of the Tiger* are an inauspicious mix of earth and wood energy; this creates inner turmoil and restlessness. These men are action-oriented, big risk-takers, tempestuous, independent and unpredictable. The 8 Gua-Tigers can be quite irresistible; you'll always feel an air of excitement around them and may get carried away by their confidence and ambitions. They are adventurous, highly social, and they have unforgettable charm! These men have energy so intense and primal, that it can overpower people. However, they are deeply sensitive and protective, never boring; but be prepared if you fall in love with these enigmatic men. They are high-maintenance and will require lots of energy and attention. The 8 Gua-Tigers crave excitement, love the outdoors, nature, and building things where their dynamic energy can find an outlet. When they move to the darker side of their nature, they can be restless, reckless, impatient, quick-tempered, obstinate, and selfish.

The best stuff: When the 8 Gua-Tigers are fully exhibiting their best qualities, they are unpredictable, rebellious, colorful, powerful, passionate, daring, impulsive, vigorous, stimulating, sincere, affectionate, humanitarian and generous. *The worst stuff:* When the 8 Gua-Tigers move to the darker side of their nature, they can be restless, reckless, impatient, quick-tempered, obstinate, stubborn and selfish.

Career: Some of the best professions for the 8 Gua-Tigers, where they may attain wealth, fame or fulfillment, as a or in Travel, Design, Politics, Police Officer, Travel Writer, Explorer, Business Executive, Acting, Property, Real Estate, Construction, Entertainment, Earthenware, Consultancy, Hotel, Insurance, Architecture, Interior Design, Pottery, Recruitment, Quarry, HR, Handyman, Farmer, OB-GYN and Clergyman.

Year of the Rabbit

The 1 Gua as a Rabbit
MEN ONLY!
Highly Sexual ● *Refined* ● *Very Clever*
Elements: Yang **Water** and Yin **Wood**

Year begins Feb 4th
Years occurring for Males: **1927**, **1963**, **1999**, **2035**
Note: No female 1 Guas are ever born in the Year of the Rabbit

Famous 1 Gua-Rabbit Men: Clint Walker, Harry Belafonte, Tom Bosley, Bob Fosse, , Doc Severinsen, Robert Shaw, Neil Simon, Pope Benedict XVI, Peter Falk, Roger Moore, Sidney Poitier, George C. Scott, Brad Pitt, Michael Jordan, Bret Michaels, John Stamos, Seal, George Michael, Dermot Mulroney, Kevin Sorbo, Marc Jacobs, Conan O'Brien, David Thewlis, Mike Myers, Charles Barkley, James Hetfield, George Michael, Donnie Yen, Jet Li, and Benjamin Bratt.

Personality & Romance: The 1 Gua men who are born in the *Year of the Rabbit* is a mix of water and wood elements, giving them lightening quick intelligence, accentuated by acute cleverness. Highly social, they are classy and refined men that are well-mannered with high style. The 1 Gua-Rabbits are low-profile, extremely tactful, accommodating and always correct and well-groomed. They are known for their good judgment and tend to be very shrewd about people and their character. These men are very concerned with how they are perceived and must have the right address, the right woman, the right kind of car; image is very important.

These men tend to be insecure by nature and are not risk-takers at all--prone to being on the cautious side of investments, relationships and feelings. They are naturally sensuous and highly sexual. The 1 Gua-Rabbits are proficient at holding on to their money, ideas, and concepts; they are also skillful at hiding secrets.

The best stuff: When the 1 Gua-Rabbits are fully exhibiting their best qualities, they are gracious, kind, sensitive, soft-spoken, amiable, elegant, reserved, cautious, artistic, thorough, tender, self-assured, astute, compassionate, and flexible.

The worst stuff: When the 1 Gua-Rabbits move to the darker side of their nature, they can be moody, detached, superficial, self-indulgent, opportunistic, and lazy.

Career: Some of the best professions for the 1 Gua-Rabbits, where they may attain wealth, fame or fulfillment, are in Art, Design, cultivation, breeding, education, religion, health care, medicine, culture, police work, judiciary, and politics, literature, public relations, law, Family Counselor, Judge, Life Coach, Adviser, Secretary, Sales, finance, banking, freight, shipping, spa, communications, entertainment, pub/bar, ice freezing, tourism, fishing, firefighting, water produce, police, sex Industry, diplomat, artist, painter, or in the publishing industry.

2 Gua as a Rabbit
WOMEN ONLY!
Quick ● *Sexual* ● *Intuitive*
Elements: Yin **Earth** and Yin **Wood**

Year begins Feb 4th
Years occurring for Females: **1915, 1951, 1987, 2023**
Note: No female 2 Guas are ever born in the Year of the Rabbit

Famous 2 Gua-Rabbit Women: Ingrid Bergman, Billie Holiday, Lynda Carter, Jane Seymour, Olivia Hussey, Crystal Gayle, Jean Smart, Jo Jo Starbuck, Melissa Manchester, Suze Orman, Kathryn Bigelow, Morgan Brittany, Cheryl Ladd, Blake Lively, Ashley Greene, Hilary Duff, Rosie Huntington-Whiteley, Ellen Page, Joss Stone and Maria Sharapova.

Personality & Romance: The 2 Gua-Rabbits are always on the alert and are very sensitive, soft and vulnerable. They tend to be honest, calm-natured, dependable, highly intelligent, clever, and their minds move lightening quick. The 2 Gua-Rabbits are generally insecure, and are not risk-takers at all. However, they are highly social, refined and classy women with superior manners and high style. The 2 Gua-Rabbits are ladies that are naturally sensuous and highly sexual. They may have unrealistic expectations such as a "Cinderella complex", and need a partner that will not take advantage of them as the disappointment could lead to depression. Since their energy is really yin, at times they may be moody and detached.

The best stuff: When the 2 Gua-Rabbits are fully exhibiting their best qualities, they are gracious, kind, sensitive, soft-spoken, amiable, elegant, nurturing, reserved, cautious, artistic, thorough, tender, self-assured, astute, compassionate, and flexible. *The worst stuff:* When the 2 Gua-Rabbits move to the darker side of their nature, they can be moody, detached, superficial, depressed, self-indulgent, opportunistic, and lazy.

Career: Some of the best professions for the 2 Gua-Rabbits, where they may attain wealth, fame or fulfillment, are in cultivation, breeding, education, religion, health care, medicine, culture, police work, judiciary, politics, Public Relations, Literature, Art, Design, Counselors, Lawyers, Advisors, Secretaries, Property, Real Estate, Construction, Earthenware, Consultancy, Hotel, Insurance, Architecture, Interior Design, Pottery, Recruitment, Quarry, Human Resources, Farmer, OB-GYN, or nuns.

4 Gua as a Rabbit
MEN ONLY!
Sexual ● *Self-Assured* ● *Progressive*
Elements: Yin **Wood** and Yin **Wood**

Year begins Feb 4th
Years occurring for Females: **1915, 1951, 1987, 2023**
Note: No female 4 Guas are ever born in the Year of the Rabbit

Famous 4 Gua-Rabbit Men: Frank Sinatra, Orson Welles, Anthony Quinn, Luther Vandross, Mark Harmon, Phil Collins, Sting, John Mellencamp, Michael Keaton, Kurt Russell, Peabo Bryson, Stedman Graham, Robin Williams, Lou Ferrigno, Dan Fogelberg, Tony Danza, Stellan Skarsgård, Rob Halford, and Treat Williams.

Personality & Romance: The 4 Guas born in the *Year of the Rabbit* is pure wood energy making these men progressive, self-assured and easy-going. The 4 Gua Rabbits are clever, highly intelligent and their minds can move quickly as lightening. These men are classy, refined, and stylish with wonderful manners. Always aware of how they are perceived, the 4 Gua Rabbits pay a great deal attention to being polished; image is very important. They can even be snobs about the status of others and their standing in the world. These men are naturally sensuous and highly sexual; they are not risk takers in love or any other area of their life. Since they may have unrealistic expectations and may be easily influenced by lovers, they need a partner that will not take advantage of them. However, free-loving women need not apply, these men will only attached themselves to women they consider having the right caliber and status; sexy sirens will not win a husband here.

When these men slip into the negative aspects of their personality they can be moody, detached, self-indulgent and superficial.

The best stuff: When the 4 Gua-Rabbits are fully exhibiting their best qualities, they are gracious, kind, sensitive, soft-spoken, amiable, elegant, reserved, cautious, artistic, thorough, tender, self-assured, astute, gentle, compassionate and flexible. *The worst stuff:* When the 4 Gua-Rabbits move to the darker side of their nature, they can be moody, detached, superficial, self-indulgent, indecisive, opportunistic, and lazy.

Career: Some of the best professions for the 4 Gua-Rabbits, where they may attain wealth, fame or fulfillment, are in cultivation, breeding, education, religion, health care, medicine, culture, police work, judiciary, and politics, Travel, Public Relations, Judge, Lawyers, Diplomats, Design Politics, Police Officer, Explorer, Advertising, Executives, Law, the Arts, Entrepreneurs, Actors, Campaigners, Education, Social Services, Medicine, Pharmaceuticals, Publishing, Farming, Agriculture, Textiles, Fashion, Technicians, Musicians, and Broadcast Announcers.

7 Gua as a Rabbit
MEN ONLY!
Refined ● *Charming* ● *Nervous*
Elements: Yin **Metal** and Yin **Wood**

Year begins Feb 4th
Years occurring for Females: **1939, 1975, 2011, 2047**
Note: No female 7 Guas are ever born in the Year of the Rabbit

Famous 7 Gua-Rabbit Men: Bing Crosby, Marvin Gaye, Neil Sedaka, George Hamilton, Enrique Iglesias, David Beckham, Tiger Woods, Tobey Maguire, Russell Brand, Michael Buble, and Johnny Galecki.

Personality & Romance: The 7 Gua men born in the *Year of the Rabbit* is an inauspicious mix of metal and wood energy; causing some internal chaos and instability. These men are diplomatic, well-mannered, shrewd, sensuous, and stylish. They are always conscious of their image, making sure that they come off impeccable. The 7-Gua Rabbit males tend to be very materialistic and could even be described as a genuine snob; having the right address, right clothes, the best associates and so forth are essential. Not known for being spontaneous, these men are careful planners in almost all areas of their life. This would include romantic relationships as well; he will only choose a spouse that in his estimation is worthy and suitable-- meeting all the criteria to secure the right image. The 7 Gua-Rabbits must be alert not to over indulge in the pleasures of life such as food, drink, money, and sex; they must keep a balanced life. While extremely charming, they can be a fast-talker, smooth talking, or have a razor-sharp tongue. These men are also naturally sensuous and highly sexual; however they will powerfully commit to the right partner. When they exhibit the darker side of their personality they can be moody, detached, superficial, self-indulgent, and opportunistic.

The best stuff: When the 7 Gua-Rabbits are fully exhibiting their best qualities, they are gracious, kind, sensitive, soft-spoken, amiable, elegant, reserved, cautious, artistic, thorough, tender, self-assured, astute, compassionate and flexible. *The worst stuff:* When the 7 Gua-Rabbits move to the darker side of their nature, they can be moody, detached, superficial, self-indulgent, opportunistic and lazy.

Career: Some of the best professions for the 7 Gua-Rabbits, where they may attain wealth, fame or fulfillment, are in cultivation, breeding, education, religion, health care, medicine, culture, police work, judiciary, politics, Farming, Estate Management, Medicine, Philosopher, Teacher, Chef, Police Office Engineering, IT, Computers, Goldsmith, Hardware, Machinery, Metal Mining, Excavation, Hi-tech Goods, Internet, Lawyer, Judging, White Goods, Metal Jewelry, Government service, Sports Equipment and Lecturers.

8 Gua as a Rabbit
WOMEN ONLY!
Virtuous ● *Materialistic* ● *Social*
Elements: Yang **Earth** and Yin **Wood**

Year begins Feb 4th
Years occurring for Females**: 1903, 1939, 1963, 1975, 1999, 2011, 2035, 2047**

Note: No male 8 Guas are ever born in the Year of the Rabbit

Famous 8 Gua Rabbit Women: Claudette Colbert, Tina Turner, Ali MacGraw, Dusty Springfield, Dixie Carter, Whitney Houston, Elle Macpherson, Brigitte Nielsen, Vanessa Williams, Nicollette Sheridan, Lisa Kudrow, Keely Shaye Smith, Tatum O'Neal, Jeanne Tripplehorn, Natasha Richardson, Charlize Theron, Eva Longoria, Drew Barrymore, and Kate Winslet.

Personality & Romance: The 8 Gua women born in the *Year of the Rabbit* are an inauspicious mix of earth and wood energy; this will trigger inner conflict and insecurities. These women are virtuous, diplomatic, modest, tactful, soft-spoken and elegant. Social acceptance is very important to them and they desire material things in the world—grand home, good marriage, successful husband who brings status, good career—the objective is to look picture perfect. Later in life, they may even become hoarders. However, the 8 Gua-Rabbits are down to earth, enjoying a life of order and peace. Their energy is quick as lightening, however they make excellent listeners and you may feel calmed in their presence.

These women may have unrealistic expectations and need a partner that will not take advantage of them. The 8 Gua-Rabbits are attracted and talented with things of the earth—real estate (especially raw land & mountainous regions), construction, landscaping and planting. These ladies will need time alone to recharge their energy; otherwise they may tend towards depression.

The best stuff: When the 8 Gua-Rabbits are fully exhibiting their best qualities, they are diplomatic, intuitive, social, refined, classy, soft-spoken, elegant, reserved, well-mannered, stylish, clever and naturally sensuous. *The worst stuff:* When the 8 Gua-Rabbits move to the darker side of their nature, they can be stubborn, moody, detached, superficial, self-indulgent, opportunistic, and lazy.

Career: Some of the best professions for the 8 Gua-Rabbits, where they may attain wealth, fame or fulfillment as or are in literature, art, public relations, judge, lawyer, cultivation, breeding, education, religion, health care, medicine, and police work.

Year of the Dragon

3 Gua as a Dragon
FOR MEN & WOMEN!
Powerful ● *Steady* ● *Outspoken*
Elements: Yang **Wood** and Yang **Earth**

Year begins Feb 4th
Years occurring for Males & Females:
1916, 1952, 1988, 2024

Famous 3 Gua-Dragon Men & Women: Betty Grable, George Strait, Grace Jones, Liam Neeson, Patrick Swayze, Isabella Rossellini, Steven Seagal, Christopher Reeve, Dan Aykroyd, Susan Dey, Mr. T, Mickey Rourke, Marilu Henner, and Jeff Goldblum.

Personality & Romance: The 3 Guas born in the *Year of the Dragon* have a mix of wood and earth giving them power and confidence, yet they are grounded as well. In the Chinese culture the mythical dragon is the most potent and revered creature, therefore it is considered one of the most auspicious signs to be born under. The 3 Gua is also an energy that exudes power, progressive and enterprising energy; the mix is indeed intense. These people have lots of energy, vigor, fiery passion, decisive and zealous ambition. The 3 Gua-Dragons feel most alive when they are inventing new things, starting new businesses, or off on a new adventure as their energy is very progressive and modern, no matter their age. When in their negative element, they can be demanding, over-bearing, too outspoken, hot-tempered and brash. However, when the creative juices are flowing they exhibit their best qualities of being loyal, dignified and generous.

In relationships they are charming and draw in their chosen partner/s with their charisma. They easily find lovers, but it's harder for them to settle down as they love a challenge even in love. When and if they marry, they will need lots of space.

The best stuff: When the 3 Gua-Dragons are fully exhibiting their best qualities, they are magnanimous, vigorous, strong, self-assured, proud, noble, direct, dignified, zealous, fiery, passionate, decisive, pioneering, ambitious, generous and loyal. *The worst stuff:* When the 3 Gua-Dragons move to the darker side of their nature, they can be arrogant, imperious, tyrannical, demanding, eccentric, grandiloquent and extremely bombastic, prejudiced, dogmatic, overbearing, brash, outspoken, violent, impetuous, and brash.

Career: Some of the best professions for the 3 Gua-Dragons, where they may attain wealth, fame or fulfillment, are as a journalist, teacher, inventor, manager, computer analyst, lawyer, engineer, architect, broker, sales person, the Arts, Entrepreneurs, Entertainers, Chef, Police Officer, Education, Bookstores, Farming, Agriculture, Textiles, Fashion, Technicians, Musicians, Broadcast Announcers, and Transportation.

6 Gua as a Dragon
FOR MEN & WOMEN!
Confident ● *Powerful* ● *Loyal*
Elements: Yang **Metal** and Yang **Earth**

Year begins Feb 4th
Years occurring for Males: **1904, 1940, 1976, 2012, 2044.** Years occurring for Females: **1928, 1964, 2000, 2036**

Famous 6 Gua-Dragon Men & Women: Dr. Suess, Robert Oppenheimer, Shirley Temple, Maya Angelou, Chuck Norris, Smokey Robinson, Bruce Lee, Frank Zappa, John Gotti, Richard Pryor, Sarah Palin, Melissa Gilbert, Wynonna Judd, Juliette Binoche, Trisha Yearwood, Ville Valo, Ryan Reynolds, Colin Farrell, Ronaldo, Benedict Cumberbatch and Blake Shelton.

Personality & Romance: The 6 Guas born in the *Year of the Dragon* are a harmonious mix of metal and earth energy; this makes these men and women very confident and powerful. They are confident, vibrant, and captivating—you will notice these people whenever they enter a room! The 6 Gua-Dragons shine in positions of leadership and authority—Senators, Governors, Entrepreneurs, CEO's, or Supreme Court Judges. These men and women play by their own rules; they also like to 'play big', no acting small or shy in the world for these lucky people. In romantic relationships, the women are very desirable, stunningly sexy with brilliant intelligence—

she will have many suitors and admirers. In order to win her heart, she will have to be properly courted and dazzled before she selects her mate for life. The 6 Gua-Dragon men have huge egos, are usually highly successful and will want a partner worth winning—a real trophy before he gives up his notoriously unfaithful ways. Both sexes need their independence to some degree; dragons can have hot tempers, they need a tough-skinned mate, but they themselves make loyal life partners.

The best stuff: When the 6 Gua-Dragons are fully exhibiting their best qualities, they are magnanimous, stately, vigorous, strong, self-assured, proud, noble, direct, dignified, zealous, fiery, passionate, decisive, pioneering, ambitious, generous and loyal. *The worst stuff:* When the 6 Gua-Dragons move to the darker side of their nature, they can be arrogant, imperious, tyrannical, demanding, eccentric, grandiloquent and extremely bombastic, prejudiced, dogmatic, overbearing, violent, over-thinkers, impetuous, and brash.

Career: Some of the best professions for the 6 Gua-Dragons, where they may attain wealth, fame or fulfillment, are as a journalist, teacher, inventor, manager, computer analyst, lawyer, engineer, architect, broker, sales person, Farming, Estate Management, Medicine, Philosopher, Teacher, Chef, Police Office Engineering, IT, Computers, Goldsmith, Hardware, Machinery, Metal Mining, Excavation, Hi-tech Goods, Internet, Lawyer, Judging, White Goods, Metal Jewelry, Government service, Sports Equipment, Clocks, Lecturers.

9 Gua as a Dragon
FOR MEN & WOMEN!
Powerful ● Brilliant ● Loyal
Elements: Yin **Fire** and Yang **Earth**

Year begins Feb 4th
Years occurring for Males: **1928, 1964, 2000, 2036**
Years occurring for Females: **1904, 1940, 1976, 2012, 2048**

Famous 9 Gua Dragon Men & Women: Joan Crawford, Greer Garson, Eddie Fisher, Burt Bacharach, Jimmy Dean, Andy Warhol, Raquel Welch, Jill St. John, Elke Sommer, Nancy Sinatra, Dionne Warwick, Lenny Kravitz, Russell Crowe, Matt Dillon, Rob Lowe, Ty Pennington, Michael McDonald, Melissa Rauch, Piper Perabo, , Kelly Clarkson, Keri Russell, Isla Fisher and Naomie Harris.

Personality & Romance: The 9 Gua men and women born in the *Year of the Dragon* are an auspicious mix of fire and earth energy; this brings great personal power. The Chinese culture revere the mythical dragon is the mightiest and most revered creatures. These men and women enjoy things on a grand scale, and play by their own rules. They are vibrant, courageous, tenacious, intelligent, enthusiastic, confident, impetuous and charismatic. 9 Guas have a sharp, brilliant intellect; they can also be wise, loyal, and sentimental. The 9 Gua-Dragon women are captivating and are not modest or unassuming—you *will* notice her as she enters a room. The male 9 Gua-Dragons have supreme egos; they are dashing, hugely ambitious, and born winners. Blessed with a fiery spirit and energy, these Guas have a permanent adventurous streak. The female 9's are usually beautiful like a diva or goddess. The 9 Gua-Dragons may have their head in the clouds at times, they are nevertheless very grounded. In the search for the ideal partner, they might find themselves often hesitating to move forward in a relationship and/or unwilling to make a permanent commitment. When they do, however, it is their intention that it be lasting. Dragons are likely to have a warm, giving personality. They can be very generous to their loved ones. Because dragons can have hot tempers, they need a tough-skinned spouse, but make loyal life partners.

The best stuff: When the 9 Gua-Dragons are fully exhibiting their best qualities, they are intellectual, magnanimous, stately, vigorous, strong, self-assured, brilliant, proud, noble, direct, dignified, zealous, fiery, passionate, decisive, pioneering, ambitious, generous and loyal. *The worst stuff:* When the 9 Gua-Dragons move to the darker side of their nature, they can be paranoid, unstable, rash, psychotic, arrogant, imperious, tyrannical, demanding, eccentric, grandiloquent, extremely bombastic, prejudiced, dogmatic, over-bearing, violent, impetuous and brash.

Career: Some of the best professions for the 9 Gua-Dragons, where they may attain wealth, fame or fulfillment, are in law, religion, the arts, entrepreneur, doctors, actors, journalist, teacher, inventor, manager, computer analyst, lawyer, engineer, architect, broker, sales person, show business, public speaking, fuel/oil, chemicals, optical, cosmetics, advertising, television, restaurants, lighting, beauty, writers, war correspondence, and soldiers.

Year of the Snake

The 1 Gua as a Snake
WOMEN ONLY!
Seductive ● *High-Strung* ● *Intelligent*
Elements: Yang **Water** and Yin **Fire**

Year begins Feb 4th
Years occurring for Females:
1905, 1941, 1977, 2013, 2049
Note: No male 1 Guas are ever born in the Year of the Snake

Famous 1 Gua-Snake Women: Joan Crawford, Greta Garbo, Julie Christie, Linda McCartney, Helen Reddy, Martha Stewart, Sally Kirkland, Juliet Mills, Vikki Carr, Ann Margret, Faye Dunaway, Nora Ephron, Sophia Rossi, Sarah Michelle Gellar, Maggie Gyllenhaal, Gaby Espino, Jaime Pressly, Katheryn Winnick, Irina Voronina, and Brittany Murphy.

Personality & Romance: The 1 Gua women who were born in the *Year of the Snake* is a mix of water and fire elements, both are volatile types of energy that makes this personality almost impossible to pin down. Usually blessed with beauty, allure, dignity and charm, these women have lovely manners and are rarely short of admirers. These women are masters at the waiting game, and they will take their time finding the right job, the right house and the right spouse. The 1 Gua-Snakes are extremely intelligent, high-strung, and know how to get what they want from people using their incredible seductive skills. It's wise not to make an enemy of this personality, they will get their revenge. They tend to be highly sexual, sensuous and emotional in nature. They are adept in using their internal energy for powerful results in all areas of their life.

The best stuff: When the 1 Gua-Snakes are fully exhibiting their best qualities, they are deep thinkers, wise, mystical, graceful, soft-spoken, sensual, creative, secretive, prudent, shrewd, ambitious, elegant, cautious, responsible, calm, strong, constant, and purposeful. *The worst stuff:* When the 1 Gua-Snakes move to the darker side of their nature, they can be a loner, bad communicator, possessive, moody, emotional, hedonistic, self-doubting, distrustful, and mendacious.

Career: Some of the best professions for the 1 Gua-Snakes, where they may attain wealth, fame or fulfillment, are as a scientist, analyst, investigator, painter, potter, jeweler, astrologer, magician, dietician, and sociologist, Public Relations, Politics, Law, Catering, Astrologer, Archaeologist, Entrepreneur, Philosopher, Sales, finance, banking, freight, shipping, spa, communications, entertainment, pub/bar, ice freezing, tourism, fishing, firefighting, water produce, police, sex Industry, diplomat, artist, painter, or in the publishing industry.

2 Gua as a Snake
MEN ONLY!
Seductive ● *Possessive* ● *Intuitive*
Elements: Yin **Earth** and Yin **Fire**

Year begins Feb 4th
Years occurring for Males: **1917, 1941, 1953, 1977, 1989, 2013, 2025, 2050**

Note: No female 2 Guas are ever born in the Year of the Snake

Famous 2 Gua-Snake Men: John F. Kennedy, Dean Martin, Dezi Arnaz, Franco Nero, Michael Bolton, Bob Dylan, Paul Simon, Nick Nolte, Jesse Jackson, Pierce Brosnan, John Malkovich, Hulk Hogan, Alex Van Halen, Keith Hernandez, Bill Pullman, Tim Allen, John Mayer, Jonathan Rhys Meyers, Travis Alexander, John Cena, Ludacris, Joe Jonas, Daniel Radcliffe, Chris Brown, and David Henrie.

Personality & Romance: The 2 Guas born in the *Year of the Snake* have an interesting combination of very earthy energy mixed with fire! Men born under these signs are grounded, sensitive, and intelligent and are masters at the waiting game. They also know how to get what they want from people, making them consummate seducers. The 2 Gua-Snake men are often soft-spoken (or use seductive speech), shrewd, cautious, calm-natured, and responsible. They can be possessive in relationships and of their possessions. Generally distrusting of everyone, they use their intuitive abilities to weed out the bad lots. One of their best qualities is how they reserve and use their internal energy for powerful results.

The best stuff: When the 2 Gua-Snakes are fully exhibiting their best qualities, they are deep thinkers, wise, mystic, graceful, soft-spoken, sensual, creative, prudent, shrewd, ambitious, elegant, cautious, responsible, calm, strong, constant, nurturing and purposeful. *The worst stuff:* When the 2 Gua-Snakes move to the darker side of their nature, they can be a loner, bad communicator, possessive, depressed, hedonistic, self-doubting, distrustful, and mendacious.

Career: Some of the best professions for the 2 Gua-Snakes, where they may attain wealth, fame or fulfillment, are as a scientist, analyst, investigator, painter, potter, jeweler, astrologer, magician, dietician, sociologist, Public Relations, Politics, Law, Catering, Astrologer, Archaeologist, Entrepreneur, spelunker, Psychologist, Philosopher, Property, Real Estate, Construction, Earthenware, Consultancy, Hotel, Insurance, Architecture, Interior Design, Pottery, Recruitment, Quarry, Human Resources, Handyman, Farmer, OB-GYN, Monks, & Clergyman.

4 Gua as a Snake
WOMEN ONLY!
Seductive ● *Mystical* ● *Intelligent*
Elements: Yin **Wood** and Yin **Fire**

Year begins Feb 4th
Years occurring for Females: **1917, 1953, 1989, 2025**
Note: No male 4 Guas are ever born in the Year of the Snake

Famous 4 Gua-Snake Women: Phyllis Diller, Zsa Zsa Gabor, Lena Horne, Kim Basinger, Bebe Buell, Kathie Lee Gifford, Benazir Bhutto, Cyndi Lauper, Chaka Khan, Kate Capshaw, Mary Steenburgen, Patti Scialfa, Marcia Clark, Bess Armstrong, Joanna Kerns, Tracy Scoggins, Amy Irving, Kathleen Sullivan, Meredith Vieira, Jordin Sparks, and Hayden Panettiere.

Personality & Romance: Those 4 Guas born in the *Year of the Snake* are a powerful mix of wood and fire energy; this makes these ladies consummate seducers, even if it's innocently. These women are highly intelligent, deep thinkers, alluring, and very dignified. Often unaware of their potent attraction, they move through life casting a spell with their charm and feminine sexuality everywhere they go. If they pursue an academic or scholastic profession, they will achieve great success and fame. The 4 Gua-Snake women love exquisite things—homes, jewelry, clothes, jets—all the trappings of a life saturated in luxury and beauty. They are masters of the waiting game, and it often pays off with a brilliant marriage that brings them wealth and status. While they are flexible in ideas, they often struggle with making decisions. These women can have movie-star looks and may be obsessed with their appearance.

Progressive, but not naturally independent, they seek a partner in life that can bring them stability and status. When the 4 Gua-Snakes allow their dark side to come into play they can possessive, distrustful, remote, and self-doubting.

The best stuff: When the 4 Gua-Snakes are fully exhibiting their best qualities, they are deep thinkers, wise, mystical, graceful, soft-spoken, sensual, creative, prudent, shrewd, ambitious, elegant, cautious, responsible, calm, strong, constant and purposeful. *The worst stuff:* When the 4 Gua-Snakes move to the darker side of their nature, they can be a loner, bad communicator, wishy-washy, possessive, hedonistic, indecisive, self-doubting, distrustful and mendacious.

Career: Some of the best professions for the 4 Gua-Snakes, where they may attain wealth, fame or fulfillment, are as a scientist, analyst, investigator, painter, potter, jeweler, astrologer, dietician, sociologist, Public Relations, Catering, Astrologer, Archaeologist, Psychologist, Philosopher, Law, the Arts, Entrepreneurs, Actors, Campaigners, Education, Social Services, Medicine, Pharmaceuticals, Publishing, Bookstores, Farming, Agriculture, Textiles, Fashion, Technicians, and Musicians.

7 Gua as a Snake
WOMEN ONLY!
Seductive ● *Talkative* ● *Regal*
Elements: Yin **Metal** and Yin **Fire**

Year begins Feb 4th
Years occurring for Females: **1929, 1965, 2001, 2037**
Note: No male 7 Guas are ever born in the Year of the Snake

Famous 7 Gua-Snake Women: Audrey Hepburn, Grace Kelly, Jacqueline Kennedy, Katarina Witt, Brooke Shields, Sarah Jessica Parker, Linda Evangelista, Paulina Porizkova, Connie Nielsen, Kyra Sedgwick, Heidi Fleiss, Constance Marie and J.K. Rowling.

Personality & Romance: The 7 Gua women born in the *Year of the Snake* is an inauspicious mix of metal and fire energy; causing some emotional, inner turmoil. These women are highly intelligent, deep thinkers, alluring, and very dignified. Often unaware of their potent attraction, they move through life innocently casting a spell with their charm and feminine sexuality. If they pursue an academic or scholastic profession, they will achieve great success and fame. The 7 Gua-Snake women love exquisite things—homes, jewelry, clothes, jets—all the trappings of a life filled with luxury and beauty. They are masters of the waiting game, and it often pays off with a brilliant marriage that brings them wealth and status. These women are often irresistible and men can fall passionately in love with; they tend to be youthful in behavior or appearance. These women are comfortable with a lot of 'stage' and are good at acting, speaking, in front of the camera or on the radio. In romantic relationships, the 7 Gua-Snakes enjoy being wooed and lavished with attention. In marriage they make good partners with no particular need for deep independence, rather security is what they crave. When they move into the negative side of their nature they can be sharp-tongued, possessive, hedonistic, self-doubting, distrustful, and mendacious.

The best stuff: When the 7 Gua-Snakes are fully exhibiting their best qualities, they are deep thinkers, wise, mystic, graceful, soft-spoken, sensual, creative, prudent, shrewd, ambitious, elegant, cautious, responsible, calm, strong, constant and purposeful. *The worst stuff:* When the 7 Gua-Snakes move to the darker side of their nature, they can be a loner, bad communicator, possessive, hedonistic, self-doubting, distrustful and mendacious.

Career: Some of the best professions for the 7 Gua-Snakes, where they may attain wealth, fame or fulfillment, are in scientist, analyst, investigator, painter, potter, jeweler, astrologer, magician, dietician, sociologist, Farming, Estate Management, Medicine, Philosopher, Teacher, Chef, Police Office Engineering, IT, Computers, Goldsmith, Hardware, Machinery, Metal Mining, Excavation, Hi-tech Goods, Internet, Lawyer, Judging, White Goods, Metal Jewelry, Government service, Sports Equipment, Clocks, Lecturers.

8 Gua as a Snake
MEN ONLY!
Seducers ● *Intelligent* ● *Sensitive*
Elements: Yang **Earth** and Yin **Fire**

Year begins Feb 4th
Years occurring for Males: **1929, 1965, 2001, 2037**
Note: No female 8 Guas are ever born in the Year of the Snake

Famous 8 Gua Snake Men: Ike Jones, Christopher Plummer, Bob Newhart, Max von Sydow, André Previn, Salman Khan, Slash, Robert Downey Jr., Chris Rock, Martin Lawrence, Dougray Scott, Scottie Peppin, Kevin James and Shahrukh Khan.

Personality & Romance: The 8 Gua men born in the *Year of the Snake* are a mix of earth and fire energy; this auspicious mix brings lots of personal power. These men are sensitive, stubborn, intelligent, and they're masters at the waiting game. They can become spiritual seekers, and trek the mountains in search of 'answers' and to find themselves. They are consummate seducers, and in relationships with lovers and partners tend to be possessive and jealous. One of their best qualities is how they reserve and use their internal energy for powerful results. The 8 Gua-Snakes tend to resist change; they can deftly handle trouble without falling apart. These men work very hard; however, they have a tendency to get bored routine and will regularly job hop. They are great thinkers and solving complex problems is stimulating to them; they do well under pressure and deadlines. They are geared for success and often become very rich with worldly honors, recognition and status.

The best stuff: When the 8 Gua-Snakes are fully exhibiting their best qualities, they are deep thinkers, wise, mystic, sensual, creative, shrewd, ambitious, elegant, cautious, responsible, calm, strong, dependable and purposeful.

The worst stuff: When the 8 Gua-Snakes move to the darker side of their nature, they can be hoarders, stubborn, self-righteous, short-tempered, a bad communicator, possessive, hedonistic, self-doubting, distrustful, and mendacious.

Career: Some of the best professions for the 8 Gua-Snakes, where they may attain wealth, fame or fulfillment, are in or as a scientist, analyst, investigator, painter, potter, jeweler, astrologer, magicians, dietician, sociologist, politics, law, entrepreneur, Philosopher, Property, Real Estate, Construction, Earthenware, Consultancy, psychologist, Hotel, Insurance, Architecture, Interior Design, Pottery, Recruitment, Quarry, HR, Handyman, Farmer, OB-GYN, and religion.

Year of the Horse

The 1 Gua as a Horse
MEN ONLY!
Confident ● *Proud* ● *Intelligent*
Elements: Yang **Water** and Yang **Fire**

Year begins Feb 4th
Years occurring for Males: **1918, 1954, 1990, 2026**
Note: No female 1 Guas are ever born in the Year of the Horse

Famous 1 Gua-Horse Men: Nelson Mandela, Eddy Arnold, Leonard Bernstein, Howard Cosell, William Holden, Denzel Washington, Ron Howard, Dennis Quaid, Ray Liotta, Jermaine Jackson, Elvis Costello, Adam Ant, David Lee Roth, Chris Noth, Yanni, Al Roker, Stone Phillips, Dennis Haysbert, Bruce Hornsby, Jerry Seinfeld, James Belushi, Ang Lee, and Dev Patel.

Personality & Romance: The 1 Gua born in the *Year of the Horse* is a mix of water and fire elements, both unpredictable energies that can be powerful and yet unstable. The 1 Gua-Horse personalities are that of strength and persistence. They are highly intelligent, high-speed and analytical thinkers, but deep inside they have a rich emotional and varied landscape.

These men have tremendous inner confidence, love to be the center of attention and are stimulated by the next challenge. The 1 Gua Horses are proud and independent but still long for a life partner who can match their deeply sensuous nature.

They prefer to live in harmony with a good mate that can bring stability and where they can exhibit their full power and spirit. The 1 Gua-Horse men tend to fall hard and fast in relationships but get a great deal mellower late in life.

The best stuff: When the 1 Gua-Horses are fully exhibiting their best qualities, they are cheerful, popular, quick-witted, changeable, earthy, perceptive, talkative, agile both mentally and physically, magnetic, intelligent, astute, flexible, open-minded and intelligent.

The worst stuff: When the 1 Gua-Horses move to the darker side of their nature, they can be moody, fickle, anxious, rude, gullible, stubborn, lack perseverance and emotionally unstable.

Career: Some of the best professions for the 1 Gua-Horses, where they may attain wealth, fame or fulfillment, are in sales, publicist, journalist, language instructor, translator, bartender, performer, tour operator, pilot, librarian, Politics, Sports, Construction, Geographer, Actor, Artists, Executive, finance, banking, freight, shipping, spa, communications, entertainment, pub/bar, ice freezing, tourism, fishing, firefighting, water produce, police, sex Industry, diplomat, artist, painter, or in the publishing industry.

2 Gua as a Horse
WOMEN ONLY!
Persistent ● *Confident* ● *Magnetic*
Elements: Yin **Earth** and Yang **Fire**

Year begins Feb 4th
Years occurring for Females: **1942, 1978, 2014**
Note: No male 2 Guas are ever born in the Year of the Horse

Famous 2 Gua-Horse Women: Josephine Baker, Jean Shrimpton, Carole King, Sandra Dee, Penny Marshall, Annette Funicello, Linda Evans, Aretha Franklin, Carole King, Geneviève Bujold, Rachael McAdams, Katie Holmes, Katherine Heigl, Maria Menounos, Ginnifer Goodwin, Nicole Scherzinger, Stana Katic, Zoe Saldana and Karina Smirnoff.

Personality & Romance: The 2 Guas women born in the *Year of the Horse* bring a powerful combination of earth and fire energy making them both grounded and exciting to be around! They thrive on being the center of attention, have incredible inner confidence, and are always looking to be stimulated by the next big thing or challenge. The 2 Gua-Horses are very proud, calm, dependable and supportive of all in their inner circle. However, they need their independence even when they choose a life partner. They strive to live in harmony with a good mate where they feel anchored whereby they can unleash their full potential. While they may fall hard and fast in relationships, they do mellow out as they age. If they are not fully able to influence their life and living environment, they tend towards depression and melancholy episodes.

The best stuff: When the 2 Gua-Horses are fully exhibiting their best qualities, they are nurturing, cheerful, popular, quick-witted, changeable, earthy, perceptive, talkative, agile both mentally and physically, magnetic, intelligent, astute, flexible, and open-minded. *The worst stuff:* When the 2 Gua-Horses move to the darker side of their nature, they can be stubborn, fickle, anxious, rude, depressed, gullible, lack stability and perseverance.

Career: Some of the best professions for the 2 Gua-Horses, where they may attain wealth, fame or fulfillment, are as a publicist, sales representative, journalist, language instructor, translator, bartender, performer, tour operator, pilot, librarian, Politics, Sports, Explorer, Geographer, Actor, Artist, Advertising, Sales Executive, Property, Real Estate, spelunker, Construction, Earthenware, Consultancy, Hotel, Insurance, Architecture, and Interior Design.

4 Gua as a Horse
MEN ONLY!
Strength ● *Proud* ● *Earthy Sensuality*
Elements: Yin **Wood** and Yang **Fire**

Year begins Feb 4th
Years occurring for males: **1942, 1978, 2014, 2050**
Note: No female 4 Guas are ever born in the Year of the Horse

Famous 4 Gua-Horse Men: Billy Wilder, Jimi Hendrix, Brian Jones, Isaac Hayes, Brian Wilson, Wayne Newton, Billy Connolly, Jerry Garcia, Larry Flynt, Roger Ebert, Calvin Klein, Ian McShane, Enrique Iglesias, Lou Reed, Ian Somerhalder, Josh Hartnett, Usher Raymond, James Franco, and Kobe Bryant.

Personality & Romance: The 4 Gua men born in the *Year of the Horse* are a powerful mix of wood and fire; this energy gives them a remarkable drive in life. They also have strength, persistence, inner confidence and a very proud air. The 4-Gua Horses can be very restless, always needing something to do or a project to start. Deeply honest, he may be a man of few words who values people being direct and forthcoming. These men have immense energy, but they are not aggressive, though they do come across as being strong and macho. They are attracted to sophisticated women who are a bit glamorous. When they fall in love, it is hard and fast- and forever. The 4 Gua Horse men can carry a torch for years for the same woman and they enjoy being the leader in a relationship.

They have a wonderful, earthy sensuality and tend to be very faithful in a romantic relationship; seldom if ever, do they stray from their chosen mate. When these men exhibit the darker side of their nature they can be fickle, gullible, stubborn, and headstrong.

The best stuff: When the 4 Gua-Horses are fully exhibiting their best qualities, they are cheerful, popular, quick-witted, changeable, earthy, perceptive, talkative, agile both mentally and physically, magnetic, intelligent, astute, flexible and open-minded. *The worst stuff:* When the 4 Gua-Horses move to the darker side of their nature, they can be fickle, anxious, rude, gullible, stubborn, indecisive, lack stability and perseverance.

Career: Some of the best professions for the 4 Gua-Horses, where they may attain wealth, fame or fulfillment, are as a publicist, sales representative, journalist, language instructor, translator, bartender, performer, tour operator, librarian, pilot, Politics, Sports, Construction Geographer, Actor, Advertising, Law, the Arts, Entrepreneurs, Actors, Counselors, Campaigners, Education, Social Services, Medicine, Pharmaceuticals, Print media, Publishing, Bookstores, Farming, Agriculture, Textiles, Fashion, Technicians, Musicians, Broadcast Announcers, and Transportation.

7 Gua as a Horse
MEN ONLY!
Independent ● *Magnetic* ● *Talkative*
Elements: Yin **Metal** and Yang **Fire**

Year begins Feb 4th
Years occurring for Females: **1930, 1966, 2002, 2038**
Note: No female 7 Guas are ever born in the Year of the Horse

Famous 7 Gua-Horse Men: Jack Benny, Clint Eastwood, Ray Charles, Sean Connery, Shel Silverstein, Richard Harris, Mike Tyson, Luke Perry, Troy Aikman, Kiefer Sutherland, Billy Zane, Jon Favreau, Michael Imperioli, Billy Burke, Donal Logue, Jeffery Dean Morgan and Matthew Fox.

Personality & Romance: The 7 Gua men born in the *Year of the Horse* is an inauspicious mix of metal and fire energy; causing some internal chaos and instability. These men are fiercely independent, proud, outspoken and may have a firey or touchy temperament. They tend to be restless and need an outlet for their incredible energy and spirit. The 7 Gua-Horse men tend to act on inspired ideas without hesitation, often getting carried away by the excitement of something new. Because these men are often brimming with ideas, energy and time may get scattered. In romantic relationships, they love the thrill and exhilaration of romance; they may set aside their normal responsible and hard-working self to pursue the whirlwind of new emotions. However, when they settled down, they make excellent husbands and great providers. With a tendency to over indulge in the pleasures of life such as food, drink, money, and sex, they must strive to keep a balanced life. They can be a fast-talker, smooth talking, or have a razor-sharp tongue. When the 7 Gua-Horses slip into the darker side of their nature they can be rude, gullible, stubborn, unstable and temperamental.

The best stuff: When the 7 Gua-Horses are fully exhibiting their best qualities, they are cheerful, popular, quick-witted, changeable, earthy, perceptive, talkative, agile both mentally and physically, magnetic, intelligent, astute, flexible and open-minded. *The worst stuff:* When the 7 Gua-Horses move to the darker side of their nature, they can be fickle, anxious, rude, gullible, stubborn, cutting speech, lack stability and perseverance.

Career: Some of the best professions for the 7 Gua-Horses, where they may attain wealth, fame or fulfillment, are as a publicist, sales representative, journalist, language instructor, translator, bartender, performer, tour operator, librarian, pilot, Farming, Estate Management, Medicine, Philosopher, Teacher, Chef, Police Office Engineering, IT, Computers, Goldsmith, Hardware, Machinery, Metal Mining, Excavation, Hi-tech Goods, and Lawyer.

8 Gua as a Horse
WOMEN ONLY!
Confident ● *Proud* ● *Stubborn*
Elements: Yang **Earth** and Yang **Fire**

Year begins Feb 4th
Years occurring for Females**: 1930, 1954, 1966, 1990, 2002, 2026, 2038**
Note: No male 8 Guas are ever born in the Year of the Horse

Famous 8 Gua Horse Women: Rita Hayworth, Pearl Bailey, Ingmar Bergman, Tippi Hedren, Joanne Woodward, Lesley-Anne Down, Ellen Barkin, Kathleen Turner, Chris Evert, Annie Lennox, Margaux Hemingway, Halle Berry, Samantha Fox, Salma Hayek, Janet Jackson, Sophie Marceau, Cindy Crawford, Sinéad O'Connor, and Robin Wright.

Personality & Romance: The 8 Gua women born in the *Year of the Horse* are an auspicious mix of earth and fire energy; this gives them a great deal of self-assurance and self-worth. These ladies are warm-hearted and generous but they are fiercely independent; trying to control or break her spirit will not end well. The 8 Gua-Horses are champions of causes, require lots of activity, and have a desire for adventure. They have a mind of their own and are usually highly principled and moral—lying and being dishonest is not part of her character. These women are rather bossy and earthy; usually very successful, they have no need to parade around their material wealth. They tend to be hyper sensitive, complex, stubborn and dependable—making good wives and spouses only when they respect their strong, patient mate. These women also have a little of 'save the world' energy. They do tend to fall hard and fast in relationships, but get a great deal mellower late in life.

The best stuff: When the 8 Gua-Horses are fully exhibiting their best qualities, they are cheerful, popular, quick-witted, changeable, earthy, stubborn, perceptive, talkative, agile both mentally and physically, magnetic, intelligent, astute, flexible, open-minded. *The worst stuff:* When the 8 Gua-Horses move to the darker side of their nature, they can be fickle, anxious, rude, gullible, stubborn, overly sensitive, lack stability, intolerant, bossy, and perseverance.

Career: Some of the best professions for the 8 Gua-Horses, where they may attain wealth, fame or fulfillment, are in or as a publicist, sales representative, journalist, language instructor, translator, bartender, performer, tour operator, librarian, pilot, Property, Real Estate, Construction, Human Resources, Earthenware, Consultancy, Hotel, Insurance, Architecture, Interior Design, Pottery, Recruitment, Quarry, Farmer, OB-GYN and nuns.

Year of the Goat

3 Gua as a Goat
FOR MEN & WOMEN!
Generous ● *Steady* ● *Outspoken*
Elements: Yang **Wood** and Yin **Earth**

Year begins Feb 4th
Years occurring for Males & Females: **1907, 1943, 1979, 2015, 2051**

Famous 3 Gua-Dragon Men & Women: John Wayne, Katherine Hepburn, Jim Morrison, Janis Joplin, Julio Iglesias, George Benson, Penny Marshall, Malcolm McDowell, Geraldo Rivera, Lynn Redgrave, Jim Croce, Joe Namath, Jennifer Love-Hewitt, Kate Hudson, Heath Ledger, Norah Jones, Rose Byrne, Adam Levine, Coco Austin, Jason Momoa and Pink.

Personality & Romance: The 3 Guas born in the *Year of the Goat* is a mix of wood and earth energy causing some internal unrest; with a purposeful and focused life however, it is eased. The 3 Gua-Goats are extremely reliable and steadfast; even under undo pressure they remain calm. They have nurturing personalities, are generous, and sensitive to the world around them. Intensely private people, it takes some time and effort to know them. Having projects and creating new ventures is most rewarding to them. They have lots of nervous energy and need an outlet, but they often have 'too many irons in the fire'. This can leave them feeling overwhelmed, exhausted and unfulfilled. Regarding romantic love, they can be insecure or shy. They do not like to be overpowered in relationships and too many 'rules' will make them feel repressed. While the 3 Gua-Goats are at times brash and outspoken, they have kind and gentle hearts.

The best stuff: When the 3 Gua-Goats are fully exhibiting their best qualities, they righteous, sincere, sympathetic, mild-mannered, shy, artistic, organized, creative, gentle, compassionate, understanding, mothering, determined, peaceful, generous and seeks security. *The worst stuff:* When the 3 Gua-Goats move to the darker side of their nature, they can be outspoken, brash, moody, indecisive, over-passive, worrier, pessimistic, over-sensitive, and a complainer.

Career: Some of the best professions for the 3 Gua-Goats, where they may attain wealth, fame or fulfillment, are as a pediatrician, actor, daycare teacher, interior designer, florist, hair stylist, musician, editor, illustrator, art history teacher, Arts, Advertising, Design, Writing, Entrepreneurs, Actors, Philosophy, Entertainers, Education, Social Services, Medicine, Pharmaceuticals, Print media, Publishing, Bookstores, Farming, Agriculture, Textiles, Fashion, Technicians, Musicians, Broadcast Announcers, and Transportation.

6 Gua as a Goat
FOR MEN & WOMEN!
Cunning ● *Patient* ● *Creative*
Elements: Yang **Metal** and Yang **Earth**

Year begins Feb 4th
Years occurring for Males: **1931, 1967, 2003, 2039**
Years occurring for Females: **1919, 1955, 1991, 2027**

Famous 6 Gua-Goat Men & Women: Eva Gabor, Eva Perón, James Dean, Ike Turner, Larry Hagman, William Shatner, Reba McEntire, Isabelle Adjani, Tanya Roberts, Connie Sellecca, Iman, Debra Winger, Vin Diesel, Jason Statham, Tim McGraw, Jamie Foxx, Criss Angel, Keith Urban, Rufus Sewell, Matt LeBlanc, Vanilla Ice, Liev Schreiber, Jimmy Kimmel, Rhys Ifans, Emma Roberts and Jamie Lynn Spears.

Personality & Romance: The 6 Guas born in the *Year of the Goat* are a harmonious mix of metal and earth energy; these men and women are cunning, long-suffering, outwardly innocent, self-disciplined and dignified. The 6 Gua-Goats are immensely creative in manipulating things, circumstances and people for advantageous outcomes. They are cunning and crafty but will give the aura of innocence or detachment; do not make an enemy of these people as they will patiently and seemingly blameless, *annihilate* you. You will not see this coming as they are famous for avoiding confrontations and arguments; even if they are in positions of authority where their will may be imposed. The 6 Gua Goat women are supremely feminine and deceptively compliant—however she is not a push-over or empty-headed. These women are powerful, ethereally beautiful and serene. The 6 Gua Goat men desire power and are ambitious, unpredictable, adventurous and at times, ruthless. In romantic relationships, these men and women, are patient and may involve schemes and dreams to find the right life partner. Intensely private people, it takes some time and effort to know them. When the 6 Gua-Goats move into the negative aspects of their personality they can be indecisive, pessimistic, complaining, and moody.

The best stuff: When the 6 Gua-Goats are fully exhibiting their best qualities, they are righteous, sincere, sympathetic, mild-mannered, shy, artistic, creative, gentle, compassionate, understanding, mothering, determined, peaceful, generous, and they seek security. *The worst stuff:* When the 6 Gua-Goats move to the darker side of their nature, they can be moody, indecisive, over-passive, worrier, pessimistic, over-sensitive and a complainer.

Career: Some of the best professions for the 6 Gua-Goats, where they may attain wealth, fame or fulfillment, are as a pediatrician, actor, daycare teacher, interior designer, florist, hair stylist, musician, editor, illustrator, art history teacher, Farming, Estate Management, Medicine, Philosopher, Teacher, Chef, Police Office Engineering, IT, Computers, Goldsmith, Hardware, Machinery, Metal Mining, Excavation, Hi-tech Goods, Internet, Lawyer, Judging, White Goods, Metal Jewelry, Government service, Sports Equipment and Lecturers.

9 Life Gua as a Goat
FOR MEN & WOMEN!
Gentle ● *Cunning* ● *Classy*
Elements: Yin **Fire** and Yin **Earth**

Year begins Feb 4th
Years occurring for Males: **1919, 1955, 1991, 2027**
Years occurring for Females: **1931, 1967, 2003, 2039**

Famous 9 Gua Goat Men & Women: Nat 'King' Cole, Liberace, Angie Dickinson, Leslie Caron, Rita Moreno, Della Reese, Steve Jobs, Billy Idol, Tom Bergeron, Gary Sinise, Kelsey Grammer, Yun-Fat Chow, Willem Dafoe, Jeff Daniels, Dana Carvey, Pamela Anderson, Courtney Thorne-Smith, Anna Nicole Smith, Toni Braxton, Julia Roberts, Carrie-Anne Moss, Kristen Johnston, Joely Fisher, Rebecca Ramos, Mitchel Musso, Jason Dolley and Hunter Hayes.

Personality & Romance: The 9 Gua men and women born in the *Year of the Goat* are a mix of fire and earth energy; this gives them inner confidence and stability. They are shy, gentle, calm, intelligent, cunning, charming, crafty, sympathetic, and tend to be dreamers. While they love being social, they do not crave attention as they prefer to be observant and autonomous; being just as happy to be left alone or to stay at home. The 9 Gua-Goats like to be fashionable and will spend money on presenting a first-class appearance; however they are rarely snobbish even when they have tons of material wealth and the finer things in life. 9 Guas have a sharp, brilliant intellect; they can also be wise, loyal, and sentimental. The 9 Gua-Goat women are usually very beautiful like a diva or goddess and may even have an ethereal air about her. These men and women are extremely reliable and steadfast; even under undo pressure they remain calm. They have nurturing personalities and are very giving people; intensely private, it takes some time and effort to know them. They have a small circle of friends, but will work hard for friends and loved ones.

The best stuff: When the 9 Gua-Goats are fully exhibiting their best qualities, they are righteous, sincere, sympathetic, mild-mannered, shy, artistic, creative, gentle, compassionate, understanding, mothering, determined, peaceful, and generous. *The worst stuff:* When the 9 Gua-Goats move to the darker side of their nature, they can be crafty, cunning, moody, indecisive, over-passive, worrier, pessimistic, over-sensitive, and a complainer.

Career: Some of the best professions for the 9 Gua-Goats, where they may attain wealth, fame or fulfillment, are in law, religion, the arts, entrepreneur, doctors, actors, journalist, teacher, inventor, manager, computer analyst, lawyer, engineer, architect, broker, sales person, show business, public speaking, fuel/oil, chemicals, optical, cosmetics, advertising, television, restaurants, lighting, beauty, writers, war correspondence, and soldiers.

Year of the
Monkey

The 1 Gua as a Monkey
WOMEN ONLY!
Quick ● Highly Intelligent ● Sexual
Element: Yang **Water** and Yang **Metal**

Year begins Feb 4th
Years occurring for Females: **1932, 1968, 2004, 2040**
Note: No male 1 Guas are ever born in the Year of the Monkey

Famous 1 Gua-Monkey Women: Elizabeth Taylor, Debbie Reynolds, Loretta Lynn, Patsy Cline, Ellen Burstyn, Catherine Bell, Vanessa Marcil, Stephanie Seymour, Yasmine Bleeth, Helena Christensen, Lucy Lawless, Gillian Anderson, Patricia Arquette, Ricki Lake, Naomi Watts, Lucy Lui, Ashley Judd, Rachel Ray, Lisa Marie Presley, and Debra Messing.

Personality & Romance: The 1 Gua born in the *Year of the Monkey* is water and metal energy, making it mercurial in nature. These women's personalities can be moody, quick, highly intelligent and at certain times of their life, promiscuous, as they can get easily bored with their lovers. The 1 Gua Monkeys are always hatching new ideas, concepts or inventing new systems.

They are playful and may be hard to pin down in relationships, they won't settle down quickly. However, with an excellent partner, they will commit to that person in every way. The 1 Gua-Monkey ladies can be secretive, could have arcane aspects to their lives or may live a whole other life.

The best stuff: When the 1 Gua-Tigers are fully exhibiting their best qualities, they are inventive, motivators, improviser, quick-witted, inquisitive, flexible, innovative, problem solver, self-assured, sociable, polite, dignified, competitive, objective, factual and intellectual. *The worst stuff:* When the 1 Gua-Tigers move to the darker side of their nature, they can be egotistical, vain, selfish, cunning, jealous, and suspicious.

Career: Some of the best professions for the 1 Gua-Monkeys, where they may attain wealth, fame or fulfillment, are in the Media, Management, accounting and banking, science, engineering, stock market trading, air traffic control, film directing, jewelry, Public Relations, Surveyor, Event Planner, Politics, Sports, Construction, Geographer, Actor, Artists, Executive, Sales finance, banking, freight, shipping, spa, communications, entertainment, pub/bar, ice freezing, tourism, fishing, firefighting, water produce, police, sex Industry, diplomat, artist, painter, or in the publishing industry.

2 Gua as a Monkey
MEN ONLY!
Sexual ● *Lightening Quick* ● *Intuitive*
Elements: Yin **Earth** and Yang **Metal**

Year begins Feb 4th
Years occurring for Males: **1944, 1968, 1980, 2016**
Note: No female 2 Guas are ever born in the Year of the Monkey

Famous 2 Gua-Monkey Men: Louis L'Amour, James Stewart, Ian Fleming, Alistair Cooke, Joe Cocker, Sam Elliott, Michael Douglas, George Lucas, Barry White, Kenny Chesney, Hugh Jackman, Daniel Craig, Marc Anthony, Edward Burns, Eric Bana, Ryan Gosling and Channing Tatum.

Personality & Romance: The 2 Guas born in the *Year of the Monkey* are a mix of earth and metal and they are quick as lightening! Inside, however they are calm, steady, dependable and altogether persistent. They are fond of creating concepts that give a new spin on old ideas/paradigms. The 2 Gua-Monkeys make caring and talented health professionals as their nurturing nature coupled with their natural intuition are a winning combination. They feel comfortable in dark spaces such as caves or may have a 'man-cave' in their home in which to retreat. In relationships, they will not settle on a partner quickly and may give the appearance of being playful, promiscuous or cavalier. When they do find an excellent mate for life, they will commit 100% and be very devoted.

The best stuff: When the 2 Gua-Monkeys are fully exhibiting their best qualities, they are quick-witted, inventive, motivators, improviser, inquisitive, nurturing, flexible, innovative, problem solver, self-assured, sociable, polite, dignified, competitive, objective, factual, and intellectual. *The worst stuff:* When the 2 Gua-Monkeys move to the darker side of their nature, they can be moody, egotistical, vain, selfish, cunning, depressed, jealous, and suspicious.

Career: Some of the best professions for the 2 Gua-Monkeys, where they may attain wealth, fame or fulfillment, are in accounting and banking, science, engineering, stock market trading, air traffic control, film directing, jewelry, Media, Police Officer, Public Relations, Designer, Surveyor, Event Planner, Property, Real Estate, Construction, Earthenware, Consultancy, Hotel, Insurance, Architecture, Interior Design, Pottery, Recruitment, Quarry, Human Resources, Handyman, Farmer, OB-GYN, Monks and Clergyman.

4 Gua as a Monkey
WOMEN ONLY!
Highly Sexual ● Quick-Witted ● Modern
Elements: Yin **Wood** and Yang **Metal**

Year begins Feb 4th

Years occurring for males: **1944, 1980, 2016, 2052**
Note: No male 4 Guas are ever born in the Year of the Monkey

Famous 4 Gua-Monkey Women: Bette Davis, Carole Lombard, Joey Heatherton, Jacqueline Bisset, Diana Ross, Patti LaBelle, Pattie Boyd, Sondra Locke, Gladys Knight, Stockard Channing, Teri Garr, Jessica Simpson, Christina Aguilera, Olivia Munn, Gisele Bündchen, Kristen Bell, Christina Ricci, and Venus Williams.

Personality & Romance: The 4 Gua women born in the *Year of the Monkey* are a mix of metal and wood energy; this may cause some internal conflict, usually in the form of self-doubt. These women are of high intelligence and have lightening quick minds. Their energy is very progressive, full of ideas, concepts or inventing new things. The 4-Gua Monkey women love their freedom and may be hard to pin down in relationships; she is playful, slippery and very quick-witted. These women are generous to a fault, are interested in everyone's business, and definitely have an opinion about everything and everybody. At certain times in their life, they may be promiscuous as they can get easily bored with their lovers. However, with an excellent partner, they will commit to that person in every way. Their chosen mate must always be aware that if they feel confined or 'jailed' in the relationship, they will exit in a flash!

The 4-Gua Monkey women are unconventional, gracious, exciting, and hospitable; when they slip into the negative aspects of their personalities they can be indecisive, jealous, suspicious, selfish, cunning and egotistical.

The best stuff: When the 4 Gua-Monkeys are fully exhibiting their best qualities, they are inventive, motivating, improviser, quick-witted, inquisitive, flexible, innovative, problem solver, self-assured, sociable, polite, dignified, competitive, objective, factual and intellectual. *The worst stuff:* When the 4 Gua-Monkeys move to the darker side of their nature, they can be egotistical, vain, selfish, indecisive, cunning, jealous and suspicious.

Career: Some of the best professions for the 4 Gua-Monkeys, where they may attain wealth, fame or fulfillment, are in accounting and banking, science, engineering, stock market trading, air traffic control, dealing, film directing, jewelry, sales representative, media, Finance, Police Officer, Public Relations, Designer, Surveyor, Law, the Arts, Entrepreneurs, Actors, Counselors, Campaigners, Education, Social Services, Medicine, Pharmaceuticals, Print media, Publishing, Bookstores, Farming, Agriculture, Textiles, Fashion, Technicians, Musicians, Broadcast Announcers, and Transportation.

7 Gua as a Monkey
WOMEN ONLY!
Lightening Quick ● *Unconventional* ● *Playful*
Elements: Yin **Metal** and Yang **Metal**

Year begins Feb 4th
Years occurring for Females: **1920, 1956, 2010, 2028**
Note: No male 7 Guas are ever born in the Year of the Monkey

Famous 7 Gua-Monkey Women: Maureen O'Hara, Shelley Winters, Bo Derek, Dana Delany, Kim Cattrall, Patti Hansen, Carrie Fisher, Geena Davis, Sela Ward, Lisa Hartman, Linda Hamilton, , Paula Zahn, Dorothy Hamill, Lisa Niemi Swayze, and Koo Stark.

Personality & Romance: The 7 Gua women born in the *Year of the Monkey* is an auspicious mix of yin and yang metal; this brings a radiant inner confidence! These ladies are gracious, generous, unconventional and make a loyal and entertaining friend. They also can be talkative, lively, and nervous.

The 7 Gua-Monkey's are often blessed with very good looks, and sensuous beauty. Comfortable with a lot of 'stage', the 7 Gua's are good at acting, speaking, in front of the camera or on the radio. These women also love their freedom and may be hard to pin down; they're quick witted and will slip through your fingers at any attempt of constraint. The 7 Gua-Monkeys also have a strong tendency to over indulge in the pleasures of life such as food, drink, money, and sex, they must strive to keep a balanced life.

If your bore these charming ladies, they may move onto a new lover; however, with an excellent partner, they will commit to that person in every way. When they move into the negative side of their personality they can have a razor-sharp tongue, be egotistical, vain, selfish, cunning, jealous, and suspicious."

The best stuff: When the 7 Gua-Monkeys are fully exhibiting their best qualities, they are inventive, motivating, improviser, quick-witted, inquisitive, flexible, innovative, problem solver, self-assured, sociable, polite, dignified, competitive, objective, factual and intellectual. *The worst stuff:* When the 7 Gua-Monkeys move to the darker side of their nature, they can be egotistical, vain, selfish, cunning, jealous, excessive and suspicious.

Career: Some of the best professions for the 7 Gua-Monkeys, where they may attain wealth, fame or fulfillment, are in accounting and banking, science, engineering, stock market trading, air traffic control, dealing, film directing, jewelry, Farming, Estate Management, Medicine, Editor, Philosopher, Teacher, Chef, Police Office Engineering, IT, Computers, Goldsmith, Hardware, Machinery, Metal Mining, Excavation, Hi-tech Goods, Internet, Lawyer, Judging, White Goods, Metal Jewelry, Government service, Sports Equipment, Clocks, Lecturers.

8 Gua as a Monkey
MEN ONLY!
Lightening Quick ● *Playful* ● *Generous*
Elements: Yang **Earth** and Yang **Metal**

Year begins Feb 4th
Years occurring for males: 1920, 1956, 1992, 2028
Note: No female 8 Guas are ever born in the Year of the Monkey

Famous 8 Gua Monkey Men: Yul Brynner, Montgomery Clift, Mickey Rooney, Walter Matthau, Tony Randall, Dwight Yoakam, Chris Isaak, Andy Garcia, Kenny G, David Copperfield, Eric Roberts, Björn Borg, Randy Jackson, Joe Montana, Bryan Cranston, Sugar Ray Leonard, Taylor Lautner, and Josh Hutcherson.

Personality & Romance: The 8 Gua men who are born in the *Year of the Monkey* are an auspicious mix of earth and metal energy; they have a great deal of inner power and confidence. These men are witty, intelligent and have a magnetic personality. Although they can be playful, mischievous and love a practical joke, they are also stubborn and competitive. While these men can often be extravagant suitors—champagne, diamonds & furs--they love their freedom and will not settle down in marriage easily. The 8 Gua-Monkeys are hardworking, great risk-takers and are survivors of difficult situations usually due to their charm and enormous social skills. They have integrity and may become spiritual seekers, and trek the mountains in search of 'answers' and to find themselves. These men are fast learners and crafty opportunists; they have many interests and need partners who are capable of stimulating them. Later in life they may become eccentric or hoarders. While the 8 Gua-Monkeys tend to resist change, they can deftly handle trouble without falling apart. They are geared for success and often become very rich with worldly honors, recognition and status.

The best stuff: When the 8 Gua-Monkeys are fully exhibiting their best qualities, they are inventors, motivators, improvisers, quick-witted, inquisitive, flexible, innovative, problem solver, self-assured, sociable, polite, dignified, competitive, successful, earthy, objective, factual, and intellectual. *The worst stuff:* When the 8 Gua-Monkeys move to the darker side of their nature, they can be hoarders, self-righteous, stubborn, short-tempered, egotistical, vain, selfish, cunning, jealous, impudent, impulsive, and suspicious.

Career: Some of the best professions for the 8 Gua-Monkeys, where they may attain wealth, fame or fulfillment, are in accounting and banking, science, engineering, stock market trading, air traffic control, dealing, film directing, jewelry, sales representative, Property, Real Estate, Construction, Earthenware, Consultancy, Hotel, Insurance, Architecture, Interior Design, Pottery, Recruitment, Quarry, HR, Handyman, Farmer, OB-GYN, Monks, Clergyman

Year of the Rooster

The 1 Gua as a Rooster
MEN ONLY!
Creative ● *Trustworthy* ● *Very Social*
Element: Yang **Water** and Yin **Metal**

Years begins Feb 4th
Years occurring for Males: **1945, 1981, 2017, 2053**
Note: No female 1 Guas are ever born in the Year of the Rooster

Famous 1 Gua-Rooster Men: James Mason, Burl Ives, Benny Goodman, Steve Martin, Bob Seger, Bob Marley, Henry Winkler, Eric Clapton, Bubba Smith, Neil Young, John Lithgow, John Fogerty, Barry Bostwick, Van Morrison, Pete Townshend, Michael Nouri, Richard Thomas, José Feliciano, Phil Jackson, John Heard, Davy Jones, Joseph Gordon-Levitt, Josh Groban, Ben Barnes, and Jay Sean.

Personality & Romance: The 1 Gua born in the *Year of the Rooster* is also a mix of metal and water energy; however this mix is grounded. The 1 Gua-Roosters have the strength of persistence and formidable personal power. They tend to be very social, and are loyal and trustworthy with family, friends and business associates. Since these men tend to *tell it like it is*, the best life partners for the 1 Gua Roosters is one that understands that under their 'crowing' and gruffness lies a heart of gold.

These personalities are more transparent and less secretive than most 1 Guas. The 1 Gua-Roosters are excellent is ferreting people out, and have very sharp opinions. Filled with a sensuous nature, sex and loyalty are paramount to these sensitive, social creatures.

The best stuff: When the 1 Gua-Roosters are fully exhibiting their best qualities, they are neat, meticulous, organized, self-assured, decisive, conservative, perfectionist, alert, zealous, practical, scientific and responsible. *The worst stuff:* When the 1 Gua-Roosters move to the darker side of their nature, they can be secretive, moody, overzealous and critical, puritanical, egotistical, abrasive, and opinionated.

Career: Some of the best professions for the 1 Gua-Roosters, where they may attain wealth, fame or fulfillment, are as an Author, restaurant owner, athlete, teacher, , journalist, travel writer, dentist, surgeon, soldier, fireman, police officer, Entertainer, News Anchor, Military, Politics, Actor, finance, banking, freight, shipping, spa, communications, entertainment, pub/bar, ice freezing, tourism, fishing, firefighting, water produce, police, sex Industry, diplomat, artist, painter, or in the publishing industry.

2 Gua as a Rooster
WOMEN ONLY!
Honest ● *Opinionated* ● *Nurturing*
Elements: Yin **Earth** and Yin **Metal**

Year begins Feb 4th
Years occurring for Females: **1933, 1969, 2005**
Note: No male 2 Guas are ever born in the Year of the Rooster

Famous 2 Gua-Rooster Women: Amelia Earhart, , Yoko Ono, Carol Burnett, Joan Rivers, Catherine Zeta-Jones, Gwen Stefani, Pauley Perrette, Lara Spencer, Rachel Hunter, Rachel Hunter, Cate Blanchett, Anne Heche and Honey Boo Boo.

Personality & Romance: The 2 Guas who were born in the *Year of the Rooster* are earth and metal energy. They have a strong independent, calm and confident nature. One minute they enjoy being the center of attention, the next they want to retreat as they can be intensely private. They are naturally intuitive, loyal, trustworthy and social. Since they tend to be painfully honest with strong, often abrasive opinions, their partners and friends cannot be overly sensitive. However, under their gruffness and sharp opinions beats a heart of gold. These women can be very clear thinkers with logical, grounded and earthy energy. Their energy is nurturing and if those choose, makes them talented healers or physician. When exhibiting the dark side of their nature, they tend towards moodiness or depression—even this may be overcome with a purposeful life.

The best stuff: When the 2 Gua-Roosters are fully exhibiting their best qualities, they are neat, meticulous, organized, self-assured, decisive, conservative, nurturing, critical, perfectionist, alert, zealous, practical, scientific and responsible.

The worst stuff: When the 2 Gua-Roosters move to the darker side of their nature, they can be overzealous and critical, puritanical, depressed, egotistical, reclusive, abrasive, and opinionated.

Career: Some of the best professions for the 2 Gua-Roosters, where they may attain wealth, fame or fulfillment, are in sales, restaurant owner, hairdresser, public relations officer, athlete, teacher, waiter, journalist, travel writer, dentist, surgeon, soldier, fireman, police officer, Public Relations, Politics, Writer, Entertainer, Hairdresser, Armed Forces, Property, Real Estate, Construction, Earthenware, Consultancy, Hotel, Insurance, Architecture, Interior Design, Pottery, Recruitment, Quarry, Human Resources, OB-GYN, or nun.

4 Gua as a Rooster
MEN ONLY!
Personal Power ● *Organized* ● *Blunt*
Elements: Yin **Wood** and Yin **Metal**

Year begins Feb 4th
Years occurring for males: **1933, 1969, 2005, 2041**
Note: No female 4 Guas are ever born in the Year of the Rooster

Famous 4 Gua-Rooster Men: Willie Nelson, James Brown, Michael Caine, Quincy Jones, Gene Wilder, Conway Twitty, Lou Rawls, Triple H, Gerad Butler, , Jack Black, and Zach Galifianakis.

Personality & Romance: The 4 Gua men born in the *Year of the Rooster* are a mix of wood and metal energy; this makes him emotionally complex. These men are very much the 'rooster', showing off their beautiful masculinity every chance they get. Highly social and deep thinkers, the 4 Gua-Roosters make excellent leaders, CEO's, or anywhere they may use their potent energy being very comfortable with power. In his love-life, he can be a skillful and passionate lover which is chiefly for physical pleasure, not necessarily romantic. It is not natural for a 4-Gua Rooster man to limit himself to a single partner. Expect that he may have many sexual partners without guilt; if he does settled down, he will make an excellent provider. After marriage, while they may be lovers, they rarely desert their partners or family. Under their gruffness lies a heart of gold but when they exhibit the negative side of their personalities they can be abrasive, critical and emotionally unavailable.

The best stuff: When the 4 Gua-Roosters are fully exhibiting their best qualities, they are neat, meticulous, organized, self-assured, decisive, conservative, critical, perfectionist, alert, zealous, practical, scientific and responsible.

The worst stuff: When the 4 Gua-Roosters move to the darker side of their nature, they can be overzealous and critical, puritanical, indecisive, egotistical, abrasive and opinionated.

Career: Some of the best professions for the 4 Gua-Roosters, where they may attain wealth, fame or fulfillment, are in sales, restaurant owner, hairdresser, public relations officer, farmer, athlete, teacher, waiter, journalist, travel writer, dentist, surgeon, soldier, fireman, security guard, police officer, Public Relations, Politics, Entertainer, Military, Law, the Arts, Entrepreneurs, Actors, Counselors, Campaigners, Education, Social Services, Medicine, Pharmaceuticals, Farming, Agriculture, Textiles, Fashion, Technicians, Musicians, Broadcast Announcers, and Transportation.

7 Gua as a Rooster
MEN ONLY!
Lightening Quick ● *Promiscuity* ● *Charming*
Elements: Yin **Metal** and Yin **Metal**

Year begins Feb 4th
Years occurring for Males: **1921, 1957, 1993, 2029**
Note: No female 7 Guas are ever born in the Year of the Rooster

Famous 7 Gua-Rooster Men: Charles Bronson, Louis Jourdan, Mario Lanza, Peter Ustinov, Sugar Ray Robinson, Vince Gill, Dolph Lundgren, Daniel Day-Lewis, Donny Osmond, Christopher Lambert, Matt Lauer, Falco, Ray Romano, and Spike Lee.

Personality & Romance: The 7 Gua men born in the *Year of the Rooster* are an auspicious mix of yin and yang metal energy; this brings a steely confidence! These men are resilient, clever, and very macho; they enjoy strutting around and crowing, but under their gruffness beat a heart of gold. However, they are no 'dandy', they have substance and depth. The 7 Gua-Roosters can be amazingly creative, rebellious, productive, and use speech to their advantage; they can be a fast-talker, smooth talker, or have a razor-sharp tongue. They may be talented in imitating voices as well. These men are very comfortable with power making great leaders and CEOs,--anywhere their considerable management and organizational skills may be exploited. In romantic relationships, they tend towards infidelity; they are quite guilt-free and comfortable courting several women at a time—a real heart-breaker! However, if they do marry, they seldom desert their families and make great providers. With a strong tendency to over indulge in the pleasures of life such as food, drink, money, and sex, they must make an effort to keep a balanced life. The 7 Gua-Roosters are very social, charming, and charismatic; they create stimulating, informative conversation wherever they go. When they move into the darker side of their nature, they can be over zealous and critical, puritanical, egotistical, abrasive, and opinionated."

The best stuff: When the 7 Gua-Roosters are fully exhibiting their best qualities, they are neat, meticulous, organized, self-assured, decisive, conservative, critical, perfectionist, alert, zealous, practical, scientific and responsible. *The worst stuff:* When the 7 Gua-Roosters move to the darker side of their nature, they can be overzealous and critical, puritanical, excessive, egotistical, abrasive, and opinionated.

Career: Some of the best professions for the 7 Gua-Roosters, where they may attain wealth, fame or fulfillment, are in sales, restaurant owner, , athlete, teacher, waiter, journalist, travel writer, dentist, surgeon, soldier, fireman, security guard, and police officer, Farming, Estate Management, Medicine, Philosopher, Teacher, Chef, Police Office Engineering, IT, Computers, Goldsmith, Hardware, Machinery, Metal Mining, Excavation, Hi-tech Goods, Internet, Lawyer, and Judging.

8 Gua as a Rooster
WOMEN ONLY!
Confident ● *Purposeful* ● *Social*
Elements: Yang **Earth** and Yin **Metal**

Year begins Feb 4th
Years occurring for Females: **1921, 1945, 1957, 1981, 1993, 2017, 2029**

Note: No male 8 Guas are ever born in the Year of the Rooster

Famous 8 Gua Rooster Women: Jessica Tandy, Jane Russell, Lana Turner, Priscilla Presley, Jaclyn Smith, Carly Simon, Goldie Hawn, Rita Coolidge, Linda Hunt, Vanna White, Faye Resnick, Rachel Ward, Melanie Griffith, Denise Austin, Caroline Kennedy, Gloria Estefan, Jessica Alba, , Natalie Portman, Anna Kournikova, Jennifer Hudson, Ivanka Trump and Victoria Justice.

Personality & Romance: The 8 Gua women born in the *Year of the Rooster* are an auspicious mix of earth and metal energy; this brings purpose & great inner confidence. These ladies are hardworking, talented, charming, resourceful, loyal, honest and open; they're very comfortable with power and prestige. The 8 Gua-Roosters love deeply, when she is wounded or disappointed, will create a wall of protection against the offenders. However, she does not wear her heart on her sleeve; you'll not see a drama queen display of emotions. They generally take life seriously; and are filled with laser-sharp purpose and efficiency. These women distain snobby, superior-acting people and they are equally unimpressed with blatant social climbers. The 8 Gua-Roosters love a challenge and will tackle it with vigor, intimidation if necessary, and with her considerable power. While they are famously stubborn, they are not vindictive, nor do they hold grudges. So talented are these ladies, there is almost no profession that they can't excel in or master; and she will manage it with efficiently and resolute independence. They are geared for success and often become very rich with worldly honors, recognition and status. Prone to 'tell it like it is', they will need a partner who is not overly sensitive.

The best stuff: When the 8 Gua-Roosters are fully exhibiting their best qualities, they are purposeful, neat, meticulous, organized, self-assured, decisive, conservative, perfectionist, observant, zealous, practical, scientific, talented, social, honest, loyal, responsible and have hearts of gold. *The worst stuff:* When the 8 Gua-Roosters move to the darker side of their nature, they can be stubborn, overzealous, critical, puritanical, intimidating, egotistical, abrasive, and opinionated.

Career: Some of the best professions for the 8 Gua-Roosters, where they may attain wealth, fame or fulfillment, are in or as a sales person, restaurant owner, hairdresser, public relations officer, farmer, athlete, teacher, waiter, journalist, travel writer, dentist, surgeon, soldier, fireman, security guard, and police officer, Property, Real Estate, Construction, Earthenware, Consultancy, Hotel, Architecture, Pottery, Recruitment, Quarry, HR, Handyman, Farmer, OB-GYN, nuns and ministers.

Year of the
Dog

3 Gua as a Dog
FOR MEN & WOMEN!
Enterprising ● *Loyal* ● *Restless*
Elements: Yang **Wood** and Yang **Earth**

Year begins Feb 4th
Years occurring for Males & Females: **1898, 1934, 1970, 2006, 2042**

Famous 3 Gua-Dragon Men & Women: George Gershwin, Golda Meir, Louis Armstrong, Enzo Ferrari, Irene Dunne, Elvis Presley, Sophia Loren, Bridgett Bardot, Maggie Smith, Pat Boone, Giorgio Armani, Carl Sagan, Mariah Carey, Leah Remini, Heather Graham, Queen Latifah, Uma Thurman, Vince Vaughn, Rachel Weisz, Claudia Schiffer, River Phoenix, and Giada De Laurentiis.

Personality & Romance: The 3 Guas born in the *Year of the Dog* have a mix of wood and earth energy; this may cause some inner tension or feeling restless. They are loyal and ready to fight for the 'underdog' or to leap into action when needed. The 3 Gua-Dogs are very enterprising and resourceful, wherever they turn their attention, it is sure to thrive.

They are diligent about completing things. Blessed with lots of vigor, energy and vitality they are in their element with inventions, new ventures or being involved in the 'latest' thing. In relationships they have trouble trusting others, and are often frightened off by the dog's insecure, worrisome and anxious nature.

The 3 Gua-Dogs tend to be faithful and loyal; they do not enjoy the excitement of the chase nor do they take pleasure in jealous scenes. When they visit the darker side of their nature, they can be cynical, stubborn and quarrelsome.

The best stuff: When the 3 Gua-Dogs are fully exhibiting their best qualities, they are honest, intelligent, straightforward, loyal, sense of justice and fair play, attractive, organized, surprising, amiable, unpretentious, sociable, open-minded, idealistic, moralistic, practical, and affectionate. *The worst stuff:* When the 3 Gua-Dogs move to the darker side of their nature, they can be dogged, cynical, lazy, cold, brash, judgmental, pessimistic, outspoken, worrier, stubborn, and quarrelsome.

Career: Some of the best professions for the 3 Gua-Dogs, where they may attain wealth, fame or fulfillment, are as a police officer, scientist, counselor, interior designer, professor, politician, priest, nurse, clerk, judge, Law, the Arts, Entrepreneurs, Actors, Counselors, Campaigners, Education, Social Services, Medicine, Pharmaceuticals, Print media, Publishing, Bookstores, Farming, Agriculture, Textiles, Fashion, Technicians, Musicians, Broadcast Announcers, and Transportation.

6 Gua as a Dog
FOR MEN & WOMEN!
Loners ● *Loyal* ● *Anxious*
Elements: Yang **Metal** and Yang **Earth**

Year begins Feb 4th
Years occurring for *Males*: **1922, 1958, 1994, 2030**
Years occurring for *Females*: **1910, 1946, 1982, 2018**

Famous 6 Gua-Dog Men & Women: Redd Foxx, Sid Ceaser, Jack Klugman, Dolly Parton, Cher, Linda Ronstadt, Suzanne Somers, Sally Field, Liza Minnelli, Patti Smith, Susan Lucci, Connie Chung, Gilda Radner, Diane von Fürstenberg, Michael Jackson, Viggo Mortensen, Marg Helgenberger, Dr. Drew Pinsky, Andie MacDowell, Gary Oldman, Andrea Bocelli, Tim Robbins, Tim Burton, Kevin Bacon, Kevin Sorbo, Nicki Minaj, Jessica Biel, Anne Hathaway, Kirsten Dunst, Kelly Clarkson, LeAnn Rimes.

Personality & Romance: The 6 Guas born in the *Year of the Dog* are a harmonious mix of metal and earth energy; these men and women are affectionate, loyal, attractive, anti-social/loners and have a keen sense of justice. They are by and large, cynical of the world. However, they shine when they engage in noble, charitable works or 'feel good' causes. While the 6 Gua-Dogs are not overly ambitious or materialistic they are diligent and dedicated workers, often rising to great heights due to this. The 6 Gua-Dogs can be blissfully naïve and innocent which can make them vulnerable or even fragile in romantic relationships. Although these men and women make the most loyal and best of friends, they tend to be self-righteous; taking a great deal of pride being honest, faithful, correct and proper- that it often comes across as 'holier than thou'. While the 6 Gua-Dogs are warm & personable, they generally have a very pessimistic view of life and are always expecting the worst to happen. They make devoted and loving partners; however they do require lots of reassurance and attention in the relationship. When they exhibit their dark side, they can be cynical, cold, judgmental and 'dog' or hound you.

The best stuff: When the 6 Gua-Dogs are fully exhibiting their best qualities, they are honest, intelligent, straightforward, loyal, sense of justice and fair play, attractive, amiable, unpretentious, sociable, open-minded, idealistic, moralistic, practical, affectionate and *dogged* (determined). *The worst stuff:* When the 6 Gua-Dogs move to the darker side of their nature, they can be cynical, lazy, cold, judgmental, over-thinkers, loners, pessimistic, worrier, stubborn, and quarrelsome.

Career: Some of the best professions for the 6 Gua-Dogs, where they may attain wealth, fame or fulfillment, are as a police officer, scientist, counselor, interior designer, professor, politician, priest, nurse, clerk, judge, Farming, Estate Management, Medicine, Philosopher, Teacher, Chef, Police Office Engineering, IT, Computers, Goldsmith, Hardware, Machinery, Metal Mining, Excavation, Hi-tech Goods, Internet, Lawyer, Judging, White Goods, Metal Jewelry, Government service, Sports Equipment and Lecturers.

9 Gua as a Dog
FOR MEN & WOMEN!
Social ● *Loyal* ●*Passionate*
Elements: Yin **Fire** and Yang **Earth**

Year begins Feb 4th
Years occurring for *Males*:
1946, 1982, 2018, 2054
Years occurring for *Females*: **1922, 1958, 1994, 2030**

Famous 9 Gua Dog Men & Women: Jacques Cousteau, David Niven, Artie Shaw, Ava Gardner, Doris Day, Judy Garland, Betty White, Cyd Charisse, Al Green, Tim Curry, Alan Rickman, Keith Moon, Timothy Dalton, Donald Trump, Daryl Hall, Tommy Lee Jones, Danny Glover, André the Giant, David Gilmour, Ben Vereen, Jamie Lee Curtis, Marg Helgenberger, Andie MacDowell, and Anita Baker.

Personality & Romance: The 9 Gua men and women born in the *Year of the Dog* are a mix of earth and fire energy; this creates an inner, firey passion and stability. They are generous, faithful, loyal, pessimistic, introspective, sincere, amiable, loving, kind and devoted. Due to bearing a strong sense of loyalty and sincerity, they will do everything for the person who they think is most important. The 9 Gua-Dogs are born with a good nature; they are not inclined towards criminal behavior or to seeking gain through dishonest means. They simply require a quite life and a good family to help them forget the ugliness and evil on the earth. They are always ready to help others, even to the determent of their own interest, and when they find themselves betrayed by cunning people, they will feel shocked and hurt. The 9 Gua-Dogs are consummate worriers and are generally pessimistic about the world around them; always fully expecting something bad is around the corner. However, they have a sharp, brilliant intellect; they can also be wise, loyal, and sentimental. Whatever they focus and turn their attention to, they will develop competence; they'll always find a way to complete an assignment. In romantic relationships, the 9 Gua-Dogs require lots of emotional support and attention as they find it difficult to trust other and are often scared off by the dog's insecure, worrisome and anxious nature.

The best stuff: When the 9 Gua-Dogs are fully exhibiting their best qualities, they are honest, intelligent, straightforward, loyal, have a strong sense of justice, attractive, amiable, unpretentious, sociable, open-minded, idealistic, moralistic, practical, and affectionate. *The worst stuff:* When the 9 Gua-Dogs move to the darker side of their nature, they can be cynical, lazy, cold, paranoid, judgmental, *dogging*, pessimistic, worrier, stubborn, and quarrelsome.

Career: Some of the best professions for the 9 Gua-Dogs, where they may attain wealth, fame or fulfillment, are in education, law, social work, research, counselor, campaigner, police officer, scientist, counselor, interior designer, professor, politician, priest, nurse, clerk, judge, acting, show business, public speaking, fuel/oil, chemicals, optical, cosmetics, advertising, television, and restaurants.

Year of the Pig

The 1 Gua as a Pig
WOMEN ONLY!
Generous ● *Sexual* ● *Intelligent*
Elements: Yang **Water** and Yin **Water**

Year begins Feb 4th
Years occurring for Females: **1923, 1959, 1995, 2031**
Note: No male 1 Guas are ever born in the Year of the Pig

Famous 1 Gua-Pig Women: Rhonda Fleming, Maria Callas, Lorrie Morgan, Marie Osmond, Rebecca De Mornay, Rosanna Arquette, Sheena Easton, Sean Young, Emma Thompson, Patricia Clarkson, Kelly Emberg, Nancy Grace, Irene Cara, Mackenzie Phillips, Marcia Gay Harden, Aphrodite Jones, Jordyn Wieber, Gabrielle Douglas, and Missy Franklin.

Personality & Romance: The 1 Guas born in the *Year of the Pig* is double water making them very emotionally, sensuous, and intelligent. These women are very generous and are keenly perceptive. The 1 Gua Pigs are affectionate, highly sexual and make great partners. They possess an inner power that makes them reliable and wise in times of a great crisis. Those born under these energies are great accumulators of wealth, energy or wisdom (the pot belly of the pig).

They are studious, diligent, and compassionate. The double water of the 1 Gua-Pig females will make them very anxious, nervous and a bit high strung. These ladies love their freedom, and even in a solid marriage will need lots of space; keeping tight reins will lead to rebellion, remoteness or an exit.

The best stuff: When the 1 Gua-Pigs are fully exhibiting their best qualities, they are honest, sturdy, sociable, peace-loving, patient, loyal, hard-working, trusting, sincere, calm, understanding, thoughtful, scrupulous, passionate and intelligent.

The worst stuff: When the 1 Gua-Pigs move to the darker side of their nature, they can be naive, secretive, over-reliant, self-indulgent, gullible, moody, fatalistic, too emotional and materialistic.

Career: Some of the best professions for the 1 Gua-Pigs, where they may attain wealth, fame or fulfillment, are in medicine, entertainer, caterer, doctor, veterinarian, interior decorator, scientist, horticulturist, social worker, librarian, investigative reporter, actor, artists, executive, sales, finance, banking, freight, shipping, spa, communications, entertainment, pub/bar, ice freezing, tourism, fishing, firefighting, water produce, police, sex Industry, diplomat, artist, painter, or in the publishing industry.

2 Gua as a Pig
MEN ONLY!
Inner Power ● *Affectionate* ● *Intuitive*
Elements: Yin **Earth** and Yin **Water**

Year begins Feb 4th
Years occurring for Males: **1935, 1959, 1971, 1995, 2007, 2031, 2043**
Note: No female 2 Guas are ever born in the Year of the Pig

Famous 2 Gua-Pig Men: Hank Williams, Woody Allen, Sony Bono, Luciano Pavarotti, Bryan Adams, Val Kilmer, Kenneth 'Babyface' Edmonds, John McEnroe, Kyle MacLachlan, Magic Johnson, Tupac Shakur, Mark Wahlberg, Josh Lucas, Ricky Martin, Chris Tucker, and Paul Bettany.

Personality & Romance: The 2 Guas born in the *Year of the Pig* are a mix of water and earth that can create an inner tension. These men are honest and affectionate with a tolerant and peaceful side to their nature. The 2 Gua-Pigs are naturally grounded, confident and dependable with a calm demeanor making them everyone's friend. However, only those in the intimate inner circle will hear their true thoughts and feelings. They are highly intelligent and perceptive who are also in possession of a great inner power; this makes them invaluable in a time of crisis. They enjoy nurturing and can make excellent doctors or practitioners of alternate healing arts such as *chiropractry,* massage therapy, and acupuncture. In relationships they are loving and affectionate, yet allowing a great deal of freedom, which they too must have in order not to feel trapped. However, a little time spent in introspection will set things back in balance; some 'cave' time is important for these men.

When these men move into the darker side of the nature, they can be moody, depressed, naive, over-reliant, self-indulgent, gullible, fatalistic, and materialistic.

The best stuff: When the 2 Gua-Pigs are fully exhibiting their best qualities, they are honest, gallant, sturdy, sociable, peace-loving, patient, loyal, hard-working, nurturing, natural healers, trusting, sincere, calm, understanding, thoughtful, scrupulous, passionate and intelligent. *The worst stuff:* When the 2 Gua-Pigs move to the darker side of their nature, they can be reclusive, depressed, naive, over-reliant, self-indulgent, gullible, fatalistic, and materialistic.

Career: Some of the best professions for the 2 Gua-Pigs, where they may attain wealth, fame or fulfillment, are in as an entertainer, caterer, doctor, veterinarian, interior decorator, transportation, entertainment, retail, hospitality, Medicine, Law, Music, Writing, Research, Scientist, Horticulturist, Artist, Property, Real Estate, Construction, Earthenware, Consultancy, Hotel, Insurance, Architecture, Pottery, Recruitment, Quarry, Human Resources, Handyman, Farmer, OB-GYN, Monks and Clergyman.

4 Gua as a Pig
FEMALE ONLY!
Generous ● *Accumulators* ● *Highly Sexual*
Elements: Yin **Wood** and Yin **Water**

Year begins Feb 4th
Years occurring for males: **1935, 1971, 2007, 2043**
Note: No male 4 Guas are ever born in the Year of the Pig

Famous 4 Gua-Pig Women: Julie Andrews, Loretta Lynn, Diahann, Carroll, Christina Applegate, Thalía, Dido, Jenna Elfman, Sandra Oh, Carla Gugino, Amy Poehler, Sanaa Lathan, Shannen Doherty, and Selena.

Personality & Romance: The 4 Guas born in the *Year of the Pig* are a harmonious mix of wood and water; this makes these ladies highly intelligent and very perceptive people. The 4-Gua Pigs make very good friends as they are compassionate, supportive and devoted. These women are great accumulators—the pot belly of the pig—of wealth, energy or wisdom. Whatever work they engage in, they are diligent and generous. In the matters of love, they dream of a *Knight in Shining Amour* to sweep them off their feet. When they let go of this fantasy, which may hurt them at times, they make wonderfully affectionate and highly sexual partners to the men who deserve them. The 4-Gua Pigs are extremely reliable and wise in times of a crisis; they are always ready to support and serve their friends. When they slip into the darker side of their nature, they may be indecisive, self-indulgent, materialistic, naïve, or gullible.

The best stuff: When the 4 Gua-Pigs are fully exhibiting their best qualities, they are honest, gentle, gallant, sturdy, sociable, peace-loving, patient, loyal, hard-working, trusting, sincere, calm, understanding, thoughtful, scrupulous, passionate and intelligent.

The worst stuff: When the 4 Gua-Pigs move to the darker side of their nature, they can be indecisive, naive, over-reliant, self-indulgent, wishy-washy, gullible, fatalistic, and materialistic.

Career: Some of the best professions for the 4 Gua-Pigs, where they may attain wealth, fame or fulfillment, are as an entertainer, caterer, doctor, veterinarian, interior decorator, transportation, entertainment, retail or hospitality, Medicine, Music, Researcher, Scientist, Gardening/Landscaping, Law, the Arts, Entrepreneurs, Actors, Counselors, Campaigners, Education, Social Services, Medicine, Pharmaceuticals, Print media, Publishing, Bookstores, Farming, Agriculture, Textiles, Fashion, Technicians, Musicians, Broadcast Announcers, and Transportation.

7 Gua as a Pig
WOMEN ONLY!
Accumulators ● *Intelligent* ● *Affectionate*
Elements: Yin **Metal** and Yin **Water**

Year begins Feb 4th
Years occurring for Males: **1947, 1983, 2019, 2055.**
Note: No male 7 Guas are ever born in the Year of the Pig

Famous 7 Gua-Pig Women: Lucille Ball, Ginger Rogers, Jaclyn Smith, Cheryl Tiegs, Teri Garr, Barbara Bach, , Sally Struthers, Glenn Close, Camilla Parker-Bowles, Marisa Berenson, Danielle Steel, Elisabeth Broderick, Deidre Hall, Emmylou Harris, Mila Kunis, Emily Blunt, and Amy Winehouse.

Personality & Romance: The 7 Gua women born in the *Year of the Pig* are a very auspicious mix of metal and water energy; this brings unexpected blessings & unique gifts and talents. These women are affectionate, peace-loving, hardworking, intelligent and passionate. The 7 Gua-Pigs are often blessed with very good looks, and sensuous beauty; however they tend to be naïve and can be used by unscrupulous, immoral men. These women are very social, charming, and charismatic; they create stimulating, informative conversation wherever they go. They can be a fast-talker, smooth talker, or have a razor-sharp tongue; they may also use their voice as a way to fame. The 7 Gua-Pigs can be vulnerable in the mouth, throat or lungs and must be careful not to smoke or engage in drug use. With a strong tendency to over indulge in the pleasures of life such as food, drink, money, and sex, they must strive to keep a balanced life. When they move into the darker side of their nature, they can be co-dependent, self-indulgent, gullible, fatalistic, and materialistic.

The best stuff: When the 7 Gua-Pigs are fully exhibiting their best qualities, they are honest, simple, gallant, sturdy, sociable, peace-loving, patient, loyal, hard-working, trusting, sincere, calm, understanding, thoughtful, scrupulous, passionate and intelligent.

The worst stuff: When the 7 Gua-Pigs move to the darker side of their nature, they can be naive, over-reliant, self-indulgent, gullible, fatalistic, excessive and materialistic.

Career: Some of the best professions for the 7 Gua-Pigs, where they may attain wealth, fame or fulfillment, are in Farming, Estate Management, Medicine, Philosopher, Teacher, Chef, Police Office Engineering, IT, Computers, Goldsmith, Hardware, Machinery, Metal Mining, Excavation, Hi-tech Goods, Internet, Lawyer, Judging, White Goods, Metal Jewelry, Government service, Sports Equipment, Clocks, Lecturers.

8 Gua as a Pig
MEN ONLY!
Accumulators ● *Intelligent* ● *Affectionate*
Elements: Yang **Earth** and Yin **Water**

Year begins Feb 4th
Years occurring for Males: **1947, 1983, 2019, 2055**
Note: No female 8 Guas are ever born in the Year of the Pig

Famous 8 Gua Pig Men: Ronald Regan, Carlos Santana, Don Henley, Meat Loaf, O.J. Simpson, David Letterman, Kevin Kline, Larry David, Salman Rushdie, Stephen King, Sam Neill, Andrew Garfield, Aaron Rodgers, Chris Hemsworth and Jesse Eisenberg.

Personality & Romance: The 8 Gua men who are born in the *Year of the Pig* are an inauspicious mix of earth and water energy; this cause inner turmoil and insecurity. These men are intelligent, perceptive, affectionate, highly sexual and make great partners. The pot belly of the pig makes them great accumulators—wealth, energy, or wisdom. Although these men can be stubborn, they have a dependable steadfast nature. They tend to have a great deal of integrity and are vey attracted to all things spiritual. They can become spiritual seekers, and trek the mountains in search of 'answers' and to find themselves. Professionally, these men are industrious, and productive; with a great sense of responsibility, creativity and rich imagination, they're not afraid to try to do what interest them. They are geared for success and often become very rich with worldly honors, recognition and status.

The best stuff: When the 8 Gua-Pigs are fully exhibiting their best qualities, they are honest, gallant, sturdy, noble, sociable, peace-loving, patient, loyal, hard-working, trusting, sincere, calm, understanding, thoughtful, scrupulous, passionate, and intelligent.

The worst stuff: When the 8 Gua-Pigs move to the darker side of their nature, they can be naive, over-reliant, materialistic, procrastinator, gullible, passive, lazy, overly meek/apologetic, fatalistic, depressed and self-indulgent.

Career: Some of the best professions for the 8 Gua-Pigs, where they may attain wealth, fame or fulfillment, are in or as an entertainer, caterer, doctor, veterinarian, transportation, entertainment, retail, hospitality, Property, Real Estate, Construction, Earthenware, Consultancy, Hotel, Insurance, Architecture, Interior Design, Pottery, Recruitment, Quarry, HR, Handyman, Farmer, and OB-GYN.

CHAPTER SIX
The 64 Compatibilities

In this chapter, we will take a look at the romance potential and compare all eight Life Guas with each other. This is a mix of two people's energy. These too, are meant to be general in nature, but I think you will find them very interesting. Reflecting back on former relationships may prove to be valuable and telling. I call these unique comparisons **Life Gua Compatibilities™.**

Please keep in mind that everyone is capable of exhibiting negative, dark aspects of them at any given time. All energy, including humans, has a yin and yang aspect—this is our nature. Depending on how evolved or aware we are, will largely depend on which of the qualities we primarily show the world. We all have times we are not 'on' and we may slip into the negative dimension of ourselves. Do not be offended or focus on the negative aspects of your personality descriptions, you may already have evolved past most of things or have them in check.

These are general comparisons of the Guas with each other in either marriage or in romantic context. All relationships will have its challenges, but some seem to be easier on us than others. Being aware of the *energy* of your partner really helps you understand what drives or motivates them—in other words 'where they're coming from'. The positive and negative of us is explored here; in all 64 comparisons—being of higher consciousness (taking the high road), self-aware or evolved makes all relationships richer.

1 Guas in Romantic Relationships or Marriages

1 Gua with a 1 Gua
Elemental relationship: WATER & WATER

The 1 Gua with another 1 indicates "lovers and friends". This is a compatible mix but things can get a bit emotional at times since the 1's tend to be moody, hard to pin down and secretive. While the 1's can be good communicators, in romantic relationships they often have difficulty expressing themselves clearly and need time alone to process their feelings. However, this couple will hit it off having *like minds* and an affinity toward the intellect, developing the mind, scholarly pursuits, and hatching brilliant ideas. Sexual union will be emotional and sensuous. *This couple both belong to the East Life Group.*

1 Gua with a 2 Gua
Elemental relationship: WATER & EARTH

In general, the 1 Gua with a 2 Gua can indicate strife and conflict. Even if the couple has a long-term marriage it can be riffed with arguments and disagreements with the 2 trying to control the 1. Often these relationships end in divorce, and a bitter one at that. Even in the bedroom, there could be conflict with *"who's on top"*. On bad days—the 1 Gua can go into moodiness and the 2 will slip into reclusiveness. Taking the high road, the 2 would only offer his/her advice or opinions when the 1 ask for it. The 2 Gua would then respect the need of their partner to process emotions at their own speed and not offer their keen, intuitive insights until approached. This would allow the 1 Gua to *flow* towards the grounded earthiness of the 2. Sexual union can be rather lusty. *This couple belongs to opposite groups, the 1 Gua is East Life and the 2 Gua is West Life.*

1 Gua with a 3 Gua
Elemental relationship: WATER with WOOD

The 1 Gua with a 3 Gua is a very harmonious relationship. The 1 Gua will indeed be a supportive life partner to the progressive thinking of the 3 Gua. These two people will be very much into organizing ideas, and can be very creative together. If both step into the negative aspects of their personalities, the 3 Gua's progressive ways and raw ambition may clash with the 1 Gua's intellectual and strong intuitive abilities. Sexual union can be very compatible as well as creatively diverse. *This couple both belong to the East Life Group.*

1 Gua with a 4 Gua
Elemental relationship: WATER-WOOD

The 1 Gua with a 4 Gua is propertied to be the perfect match of energy. The 1 Gua will be totally supportive and feed energy to the 4. Under this type of attention, the 4 Gua will blossom and grow. This can be a highly sexual and romantic union, with both partners feeling the harmonic energy. These couples often enjoy tantric sexual practices. If the couple is not evolved, both can be tempted by affairs outside the union. This union has a very sexy, 'peach blossom' energy, each partner need to stay on their toes to present their best sides. Stepping into a negative energy could have the 1 Gua going into emotional, irrational behavior to sexually control the 4 Gua. Evolved couples will enjoy a wonderful, loving connection that grows more deeply over time that may put them into 'their own world'—so focused they are on each other. *This couple both belong to the East Life Group.*

1 Gua with a 6 Gua
Elemental relationship: WATER-METAL

The 1 Gua with a 6 Gua can indicate a "heavenly combination". Normally, the 1 Gua will make the 6 Gua feel drained. And when the couple is not grounded, this can *rust out* or *corrode* a perfectly good relationship. The 6 Guas are natural leaders, but often need time to "marinate" in their feelings. The 1 Gua also can be moody and introspective; wanting some time alone as well. As both partners tend to be in their head, they will need to take time to hear each other and connect in the heart. However, if the couple is evolved, the combination is good with the 6 Gua helping their partner *give birth* to creative ideas and projects. Sexual union can be compatible, and sensuous. *This couple belongs to opposite groups, the 1 Gua is East Life and the 6 Gua is West Life.*

1 Gua with a 7 Gua
Elemental relationship: WATER-METAL

The 1 Gua with a 7 Gua will indicate a great deal of sex and romance with *peachy, sexy* energy. In this relationship, the 7 Gua's natural joyfulness could turn sour as the 1 Gua's energy can be somewhat demanding. If the couple is grounded and evolved, the physical part of the relationship can be quite wonderful. Both Gua's tend to be highly sexual, but indicate that taking time to find a great spouse can be very focused and committed to the other. If not, both could be prone to affairs of the heart, unrequited love and extra martial affairs/intimate encounters. *This couple belongs to opposite groups, the 1 Gua is East Life and the 7 Gua is West Life.*

1 Gua with an 8 Gua
Elemental relationship: WATER-EARTH

The 1 Gua with an 8 Gua indicates conflict, fighting and general competitiveness. The fixed stubbornness of the 8 can try to control the 1. The 1 Gua will feel "out of control" when confronted with stubborn earthiness of the 8. Sexual union can also have frustrations and conflict, but still can be very sensuous. When both are evolved souls and are grounded, the 8 will allow his/her emotional, life partner to process without interference. The 1 Gua can then *flow* towards their "rock of Gibraltar" that is constant and noble. *This couple belongs to opposite groups, one is East Life and the other is West Life.*

1 Gua with a 9 Gua
Elemental relationship: WATER and FIRE

The 1 Gua with a 9 Gua is oddly enough very compatible, often creating "steamy" love affairs and hot romance. However, the 1 Gua can completely put out the *fiery* nature of the 9 Gua if they are not in succinct with the energy of their partners or not grounded. If the souls are spiritually evolved, the high emotions/intellect of the 1 Gua will be well-received by the brilliant, fiery goddess energy of the 9's. Sexual union can be highly charged, sensuous and create a lot of *heat* that would be apparent even to casual onlookers. *This couple both belong to the East Life Group.*

2 Gua in Romantic Relationships or Marriages

2 Gua with a 1 Gua
Elemental relationship: EARTH-WATER

The 2 Gua with a 1 Gua indicates strife and conflict. Even if the couple has a long-term marriage it can be riddle with arguments and disagreements with the 2 trying to control the 1. Often these relationships end in divorce, and a bitter one at that. Taking the high road, the 2 would only offer his/her advice/opinion when the 1 ask for it. The 2 Gua would then respect the need of his/her partner to process emotions at their own speed and not offer their keen, intuitive insights until approached. This would allow the 1 Gua to *flow* towards the earthiness of the 2. Sexual union will be intense. *This couple belongs to opposite groups, one is East Life and the other is West Life.*

2 Gua with a 2 Gua
Elemental relationship: EARTH-EARTH

The 2 Gua with another 2 indicates "friends and lovers". With the intuitive energy of the 2 Guas, they will be in tune with each other's needs and feelings. The energy is earthy, and they will enjoy hiking, gardening, earthy sex, constructing things together, and have an interest in healing arts and medicine. When this couple slips into the negative aspects of their nature, they will not speak to each other, want time alone or become depressed. Sexual union can be deep and earthy. *This couple both belong to the West Life Group.*

2 Gua with a 3 Gua
Elemental relationship: EARTH-WOOD

The 2 Gua with a 3 Gua can indicate lots of fighting and conflict with the energy of the 3 trying to control the 2. If the couple is grounded, these relationships can be quite good with the progressive energy of the 3 Gua giving direction to the feeling & intuitive 2. Otherwise, there can be constant conflict, like two bulls fighting. Sexual union can be intense, even if is not frequent. *This couple belongs to opposite groups, one is East Life and the other is West Life.*

2 Gua with a 4 Gua
Elemental relationship: EARTH-WOOD

The 2 Gua with a 4 Gua can be a difficult match. The 4 Gua will try to control the 2, often manipulating them using sex. These relationships can be tumultuous, and if the 2 cannot come to terms, divorce and break-ups are common. If they are grounded and evolved, the 4 Gua can bring a feeling of safety to the relationship and the sexual union can be quite intense. *This couple belongs to opposite groups, one is East Life and the other is West Life.*

2 Gua with a 6 Gua
Elemental relationship: EARTH-METAL

The 2 Gua with a 6 Gua can be wonderfully compatible. The 2 Gua and the 6 represent pure yin and pure yang energy, and this makes this couple very well-matched. The 6 is the real leader here with the 2 as the follower, however the 2 Gua is a complete supporter of their mates. The energy of the 2 will assist the 6 to be all they can be! Sexual union can be both heavenly and earthy all at once! *This couple both belong to the West Life Group.*

2 Gua with a 7 Gua
Elemental relationship: EARTH-METAL

The 2 Gua with a 7 Gua will indicate a very good match. The quieter, more serious nature of the 2 Gua is a good match for the more vibrant, talkative and fun nature of the 7 Gua. The 7 Gua brings beauty to the relationship, while the 2 Gua gives his/her calmness to balance things out. Sex is earthy, and highly sensuous. *This couple both belong to the West Life Group.*

2 Gua with an 8 Gua
Elemental relationship: EARTH-EARTH

The 2 Gua with an 8 Gua indicate are the "perfect match" for each other. These Guas are both earthy, with the calmness of the 2 and the noble/stubbornness of the 8. Both Guas have an intense interest in the spiritual/metaphysics and will have this as an aspect of the relationship. Sex can be earthy, playful and spiritual. *This couple both belong to the West Life Group.*

2 Gua with a 9 Gua
Elemental relationship: EARTH-FIRE

The 2 Gua with a 9 Gua is a good match. The 2 Gua is really supported and fired up by the 9's energy. The 9 will enjoy the naturally calm nature of the 2 which perfectly complements the wild, fiery nature of the 9. These energies balance and feed each other beautifully. Sexual union can be hot, unconventional and exciting. *This couple belongs to opposite groups, one is East Life and the other is West Life.*

3 Gua in Romantic Relationships or Marriages

3 Gua with a 1 Gua
Elemental relationship: WOOD-WATER

The 3 Gua with a 1 Gua is a very harmonious relationship. The 1 Gua will indeed be a supportive life partner to the progressive thinking 3 Gua. These two people will be very much into organizing ideas, and can be very creative together. Sexual union can be very compatible as well as creatively diverse. *This couple both belong to the East Life Group.*

3 Gua with a 2 Gua
Elemental relationship: WOOD-EARTH

The 2 Gua with a 3 Gua can indicate lots of fighting and conflict with the energy of the 3 trying to control the 2. If the couple is grounded, these relationships can be quite good with the progressive energy of the 3 Gua giving direction to the feeling & intuitive 2. Otherwise, there can be constant conflict, like two bulls fighting. Sexual union can be intense, even if is not frequent.

This couple belongs to opposite groups, one is East Life and the other is West Life.

3 Gua with a 3 Gua
Elemental relationship: WOOD-WOOD

The 3 Gua with a 3 Gua can indicate friends and lovers. There could be difficulty with both having the tendency to be outspoken and overly direct. However, if both are grounded this couple could enjoy open communication with each other making them closer. This couple can enjoy creating many ventures together which could enhance their natural vitality and high energy. Sexual union will be compatible, invigorating and can have many delightful surprises. *This couple both belong to the East Life Group*

3 Gua with a 4 Gua
Elemental relationship: WOOD-WOOD

The 3 Gua with a 4 Gua can be a can be a very good match. The progressive thinking with their multitude of ideas will perfectly suit the flexible energy of the 4's. Since the 4, at times, can be manipulated by their partners, the 3 Gua would need to use caution not to overwhelm his/her mate with too much aggressive energy. All in all, it is a highly compatible match and sexual union can be inventive and sensuous. *This couple both belong to the East Life Group*

3 Gua with a 6 Gua
Elemental relationship: WOOD-METAL

The relationship of the 3 Gua with a 6 Gua can be confrontational and difficult. The 6 Gua, if un-evolved, will cut down their partners especially concerning their ideas and point of views. The natural leadership/bossiness of the 6 can bring out nervousness and impatience of the 3 Gua. However, if these souls are developed and have worked on themselves, it can work out. The 6 Gua has a real opportunity here to help "carve out" the progressive thinking 3's ideas and help him/her put them into action. Sexual union can be deeply satisfying and creative. *This couple belongs to opposite groups, one is East Life and the other is West Life.*

3 Gua with a 7 Gua
Elemental relationship: WOOD-METAL

The 3 Gua with a 7 Gua can indicate strife and discord. The 7 Gua, who is usually joyous, can get his/her "digs" into their partner especially using critical words and speech. The 3 Gua would feel *cut down* and could then step into their outspoken nature and fighting would get progressively worse. If both Guas have awareness, the relationship can be tantalizing in spite of their differences. With the natural vitality of the 3 and the sensuous nature/beauty of the 7, sexual union can be wonderful and full of surprises. *This couple belongs to opposite groups, one is East Life and the other is West Life.*

3 Gua with an 8 Gua
Elemental relationship: WOOD-EARTH

The 3 Gua with an 8 Gua indicate a natural tug a war with the 3 Gua trying to wrestle control over the 8. The stubborn nature of the 8 would frustrate the 3's effort to be the controlling partner in the relationship. However, if both people are evolved souls the relationship can be deeply satisfying. The 3 Gua's deep-rooted, steady nature would mix well with the noble energy of the 8. Both tend to be organized and progressive thinkers, and *constructing* things together is the surest way of remaining close as a couple. Sexual union can be very intense, earthy and creative. *This couple belongs to opposite groups, one is East Life and the other is West Life.*

3 Gua with a 9 Gua
Elemental relationship: WOOD-FIRE

The 3 Gua with a 9 Gua are considered the "perfect match". The high-energy 3 Gua is a true supporter of the 9's fiery nature. The super intellect of the 9 and the progressive thinking 3's can be unstoppable. They are perfectly suited to capture whatever they are focused on as a couple—often this is fame for them both. If they are un-evolved, they can create a raging fire together and burn anyone in their path! Sexual union will be hot and intense. *This couple both belong to the East Life Group.*

4 Gua in Romantic Relationships or Marriages

4 Gua with a 1 Gua
Elemental Relationship: WOOD-WATER

The 1 Gua with a 4 Gua is said to be a "perfect match". The 1 Gua will be totally supportive and feed energy to the 4. Under this type of attention, the 4 Gua will blossom and grow. This can be a highly sexual and romantic union, with both partners feeling the harmonic energy. These couples often enjoy tantric sexual practices. *This couple both belong to the East Life Group.*

4 Gua with a 2 Gua
Elemental relationship: WOOD-EARTH

The 2 Gua with a 4 Gua can be a difficult match. The 4 Gua will try to control the 2, often manipulating them using sex. These relationships can be tumultuous, and if the 2 cannot come to terms, divorce and break-ups are common. If they are grounded and evolved, the 4 Gua can bring a feeling of safety to the relationship and the sexual union can be quite intense. *This couple belongs to opposite groups, one is East Life and the other is West Life.*

4 Gua with a 3 Gua
Elemental relationship: WOOD-WOOD

The 4 Gua with a 3 Gua is a good match of energy. The 3 Gua is a natural leader, while the 4 Gua is flexible, a good consort or follower. The energy can yield collaboration in progressive ideas, expansion, and beginning new things. This can be a very harmoniousness union filled with growth and vitality. Romance can blossom throughout the marriage if they take care to honor each other's unique qualities. Sexual union can be satisfying and creative. *This couple both belong to the East Life Group.*

4 Gua with a 4 Gua
Elemental relationship: WOOD-WOOD

The 4 Gua with another 4 Gua will indicate 'friends and lovers'. These highly romantic, and often scholarly people, can have a joyful union of souls. Like the 3 Guas, the 4's can also be very progressive thinkers. Even in late life, these Gua tend to be display youthful vigor and ideas. They keep in touch with the times, and are often highly physical and sexual. Needless to say that sexual union can be intense, often, and at times playful. If the couple is not evolved or deeply connected and committed to each other, there could be affairs, divorce or love triangles. *This couple both belong to the East Life Group.*

4 Gua with a 6 Gua
Elemental relationship: WOOD-METAL

The 4 Gua with a 6 Gua could be a changeling relationship. The 6 Guas often are authoritative and have powerful energy, and this can overwhelm the malleable 4. If the couple is not evolved, the 6 energy can *cut* down the natural romantic and creative ideas of the 4. And sexually, it could be masochistic or may involve roles of domination. However, with more spiritual awareness, the insightful guidance of the 6 can help mold the 4 who often tend to 'blow with the wind'. The 6 and the 4 both indicate a level of fame if desired. Couples with awareness can thrive in this union, if not; the couple could end in a bitter divorce. Sexual union can be highly intense. *This couple belongs to opposite groups, one is East Life and the other is West Life.*

4 Gua with a 7 Gua
Elemental relationship: WOOD-METAL

The 4 with a 7 Gua can be very much like the 4 and 6 Gua, it will have difficult aspects. The 4 Gua may find themselves at the bitter end of the sharp, critical tongue of the 7. The union can be rewarding if the couple are sufficiently evolved however. Then, the 7 Gua can 'carve out' the best of the 4 Gua. Creative ideas will flourish between them. Both Guas have a lot of sexual energy and a youthful take on life. The relationship can be highly rewarding when there is commitment and respect. If not, both have a tendency to stray out of boredom or not being sufficiently supported by their partner. Sexual union can be joyful, fun and rewarding. *This couple belongs to opposite groups, one is East Life and the other is West Life.*

4 Gua with an 8 Gua
Elemental relationship: WOOD-EARTH

The 4 Gua with an 8 Gua indicate a natural tug a war with the 4 Gua trying to wrestle control over the 8. The stubborn nature of the 8 would frustrate the 4's effort to be the controlling partner in the relationship. However, if both people are evolved souls, the relationship can be deeply satisfying. The 4 Gua's malleable nature would mix well with the noble energy of the 8. The romantic nature of the 4 can win over, rather than control, the stable energy of the 8 Gua. Sexual union can be very intense, earthy and romantic. *This couple belongs to opposite groups, one is East Life and the other is West Life.*

4 Gua with a 9 Gua
Elemental relationship: WOOD-FIRE

The 4 Gua with a 9 Gua is a highly compatible match. The 4 Gua provides loyal support to the 9, making them the 'giver' in the relationship. The fiery intellect of the 9 Gua is an excellent match for the romantic and often scholarly 4. On the negative side, with the indecisive 4 and the rashness of the 9, sparks can fly. These two Guas are indicative of fame, and there could be some unhealthy competitiveness if the couple is not connected. The best way for a long marriage is the meeting of minds and hearts through clear communication. Sexual union can be intense and hot! *This couple both belong to the East Life Group.*

6 Gua in Romantic Relationships or Marriages

6 Gua with a 1 Gua
Elemental Relationship: METAL-WATER
Sexy, 'Peach Blossom' Energy

The 1 Gua with a 6 Gua can indicate a "heavenly combination". Normally, the 1 Gua will make the 6 Gua feel drained. And when the couple is not grounded, this can *rust out* or *corrode* a perfectly good relationship. The 6 Guas are natural leaders, but often need time to "marinate" in their feelings. The 1 Gua also can be moody and also want some time alone. However, if the couple is evolved, the combination is good with the 6 Gua helping their partner *give birth* to creative ideas and projects. Sexual union can be emotional, compatible, and creative. *This couple belongs to opposite groups, one is East Life and the other is West Life.*

6 Gua with a 2 Gua
Elemental relationship: WOOD-EARTH

The 2 Gua with a 6 Gua can be wonderfully compatible. The 2 Gua and the 6 represent pure yin and pure yang energy, and this makes this couple very well-matched. The 6 is the real leader here with the 2 as the follower, however the 2 Gua is a complete supporter of their mates. The energy of the 2 will assist the 6 to be all they can be! Sexual union can be both heavenly and earthy all at once! *This couple both belong to the West Life Group.*

6 Gua with a 3 Gua
Elemental relationship: METAL-WOOD

The relationship of the 3 Gua with a 6 Gua can be difficult and riddled with conflict. The 6 Gua, if un-evolved, will cut down their partners especially concerning their ideas and point of views. The natural leadership/bossiness of the 6 can bring out nervousness and impatience of the 3 Gua. However, if these souls are developed and have worked on themselves, it can be rewarding. The 6 Gua has a real opportunity here to help "carve out" the progressive thinking 3's ideas and help him/her put them into action. Sexual union can be deeply satisfying and creative. *This couple belongs to opposite groups, one is East Life and the other is West Life.*

6 Gua with a 4 Gua
Elemental relationship: METAL-WOOD

The 6 Gua with a 4 Gua could be a changeling relationship. The 6 Guas often are authoritative and have powerful energy, and this can overwhelm the malleable 4. If the couple is not evolved, the 6 energy can *cut* down the natural romantic and creative ideas of the 4. And sexually, it could be masochistic or may involve roles of domination. However, with more spiritual awareness, the insightful guidance of the 6 can help mold the 4 who often tend to 'blow with the wind'. The 6 and the 4 both indicate a level of fame if desired. Couples with awareness can thrive in this union, if not; the couple could end in a bitter divorce. Sexual union can be highly intense. *This couple belongs to opposite groups, one is East Life and the other is West Life.*

6 Gua with a 6 Gua
Elemental relationship: METAL-METAL

The 6 Gua with another 6 Gua can be considered a desirable match. However, it is not without its difficult aspect. Both parties have powerful, authoritative energy and when they butt heads, it will be about belief systems, ideas and the perspectives each holds. Both tend to over think things and both have the energy to lead people. Sexual union could be blissful, imaginative and may involve fun, role-playing. *This couple both belong to the West Life Group.*

6 Gua with a 7 Gua
Elemental relationship: METAL-METAL

The 6 Gua with a 7 Gua is considered one of the "perfect matches" but can be clashing at the same time. In very traditional terms, it means the older man with the younger woman. The natural playfulness of the 7 may get on the nerves of the more serious, self-absorbed and over-thinking 6 Gua. As the charismatic 7 is prone to indulge in excess, the 6 Gua could be tempted to boss or correct their mate. If the couple were evolved however, the match can be very rewarding. They could create successful businesses that may involve products of sensuality, jewelry, travel, or metaphysics. Sexual union could be very expressive, non-traditional, and involve playful 'dirty talk'. *This couple both belong to the West Life Group.*

6 Gua with a 8 Gua
Elemental relationship: METAL-EARTH

The 6 Gua matched with an 8 Gua is considered very compatible energy. The steady and noble energy of the 8 is a good compliment to the authoritative energy of the 6. This is heaven and earth energy, however at times the 6 Gua can slightly deplete the 8 who would be the supporter in the relationship. On a more negative note, un-evolved 8's can be hoarders, and the 6 can be self-absorbed—this would cause a great deal of conflict. If the souls were very developed and clear, the match can have heavenly aspects with both people leaning to things spiritual. Sexual union can be deep, earthy and extremely connected. *This couple both belong to the West Life Group.*

6 Gua with a 9 Gua
Elemental relationship: METAL-FIRE

In general, the match of a 6 Gua with a 9 Gua is not a compatible and could be difficult. Nevertheless, they will be attracted by their shared high intellect and thinking power. The 9's can totally 'melt' down the energy of the 6; naturally this will cause a conflict with the 6 whose nature is to rule and exert power. Sparks could fly, sharp words and hot debates over ideas could happen on a regular basis. However, if both people are advanced in consciousness, the union can be quite titillating and exciting with a spectacular exchange of ideas—a true power couple. Sexual union can be just as exciting with each submitting to their passionate natures. *This couple belongs to opposite groups, one is East Life and the other is West Life.*

7 Gua in Romantic Relationships or Marriage

7 Gua with a 1 Gua
Elemental Relationship: METAL-WATER
Sexy, 'Peach Blossom' Energy

The 1 Gua with a 7 Gua will indicate a great deal of sex and romance with *peachy* energy, sweet and juicy. In this relationship, the 7 Gua's natural joyfulness could turn sour as the 1 Gua's energy can be somewhat demanding. If the couple is grounded, the physical part of the relationship can be quite wonderful. If not, both could be prone to affairs of the heart and even step out of the marriage for what their hearts long for. *This couple belongs to opposite groups, one is East Life and the other is West Life.*

7 Gua with a 2 Gua
Elemental relationship: METAL-EARTH

The 2 Gua with a 7 Gua will indicate a very good match. The quieter, more serious nature of the 2 Gua is a good match for the more vibrant, talkative and fun nature of the 7 Gua. The 7 Gua brings beauty to the relationship, while the 2 Gua gives his/her calmness to balance things out. Sex is earthy, and highly sensuous. *This couple both belong to the West Life Group.*

7 Gua with a 3 Gua
Elemental relationship: METAL-WOOD

The 3 Gua with a 7 Gua can indicate strife and discord. The 7 Gua, who is usually joyous, can get his/her "digs" into their partner especially using critical words and speech. The 3 Gua would feel *cut down* and could then step into their outspoken nature and fighting would get progressively worse. If both Guas have awareness and are evolved, the relationship can be tantalizing in spite of their differences. With the natural vitality of the 3 and the sensuous nature/beauty of the 7, sexual union can be wonderful and full of surprises. *This couple belongs to opposite groups, one is East Life and the other is West Life.*

7 Gua with a 4 Gua
Elemental relationship: METAL-WOOD

The 4 with a 7 Gua can be very much like the 4 and 6 Gua, it will have difficult aspects. The 4 Gua may find themselves at the bitter end of the sharp, critical tongue of the 7. The union can be rewarding if the couple are sufficiently evolved however. Then, the 7 Gua can 'carve out' the best of the 4 Gua. Creative ideas will flourish between them. Both Guas have a lot of sexual energy and a youthful take on life. The relationship can be highly rewarding when there is commitment and respect. If not, both have a tendency to stray out of boredom or not being sufficiently supported by their partner. Sexual union can be joyful, fun and rewarding. *This couple belongs to opposite groups, one is East Life and the other is West Life.*

7 Gua with a 6 Gua
Elemental relationship: METAL-METAL

The 6 Gua with a 7 Gua is considered both compatible and clashing at the same time; it is one of the 'perfect matches". In very traditional terms, it means the younger woman with an older man. The natural playfulness of the 7 may get on the nerves of the more serious, self-absorbed and over-thinking 6 Gua. As the charismatic 7 is prone to indulge in excess, the 6 Gua could be tempted to boss or correct their mate, if this is the man in the relationship, it is doubly so. If the couple were evolved, the match can be very rewarding. They could create successful businesses that may involve products of sensuality, jewelry, travel, or metaphysics. Sexual union could be very expressive, non-traditional, and involve 'dirty talk'. *This couple both belong to the West Life Group.*

7 Gua with a 7 Gua
Elemental relationship: METAL-METAL

This is considered a highly compatible match of lovers and friends. If the couple is not evolved, there could be too much indulgence in the pleasures of life, and the couple could exhaust and loose themselves in pursuing them. With no counterbalance or grounding energy, there could be over-spending, flirtations, and too many parties. However, if the couple is highly developed they could both be attracted to spiritual and metaphysical interests. They could be speakers and champions of human concerns, planetary issues, and political rightness. Sexual union can be playful and highly sensuous with possible interests in the tantric practices. *This couple both belong to the West Life Group.*

7 Gua with a 8 Gua
Elemental relationship: METAL-EARTH

The 7 Gua with an 8 Gua is excellent and considered very well-matched. The earthiness of the 8 grounds the nervous energy of the 7. The 7 brings the beauty and liveliness to the relationship, as the 8's can be more serious and stubborn. However, the 8 is considered the 'giver' in the relationship as the 7 does slightly deplete their energy. If the 8 is not developed they will lean towards greed, and the 7 will go to excesses and affairs. Sexual union can be highly sensuous, earthy and deeply gratifying for both parties. *This couple both belong to the West Life Group.*

7 Gua with a 9 Gua
Elemental relationship: METAL-FIRE

In general, the 7 Gua matched up with a 9 Gua is considered extremely negative and ill-suited. The 9 may try to control their partner with their passionate opinions and ideas, and the 7 will rebel using their sharp tongues. If not sufficiently evolved, conflict could be a daily event. However, if they are advanced in consciousness, the relationship can be exciting on several levels—the intellect, sexual, and spiritual. Both the 9 and the 7 bring passion, sensuousness, and brilliance. These Guas can be a powerful couple when the energy is directed to the greater good. Sexual union can be intense, beautiful and deeply sensual. *This couple belongs to opposite groups, one is East Life and the other is West Life.*

8 Gua in Romantic Relationships or Marriages

8 Gua with a 1 Gua
Elemental relationship: METAL-WATER

The 8 Gua with an 1 Gua indicates conflict, fighting and general competitiveness. The fixed stubbornness of the 8 can try to control the 1. The 1 Gua will feel "out of control" when confronted with mountain earthiness of the 8. Sexual union can also have frustrations and conflict, but still can be very sensuous. When both are evolved souls and are grounded, the 8 will allow his/her emotional life partner to process without interference. The 1 Gua can then *flow* towards their "rock of Gibraltar" that is constant and noble. *This couple belongs to opposite groups, one is East Life and the other is West Life.*

8 Gua with a 2 Gua
Elemental relationship: EARTH-EARTH

The 8 Gua with an 2 Gua indicate are the "perfect match" for each other. These Guas are both earthy, with the calmness of the 2 and the noble/stubbornness of the 8. Both Guas have an intense interest in the spiritual/metaphysics and will have this as an aspect of the relationship. Sex can be earthy, playful and spiritual. *This couple both belong to the West Life Group.*

8 Gua with a 3 Gua
Elemental relationship: EARTH-WOOD

The 8 Gua with an 3 Gua indicate a natural tug a war with the 3 Gua trying to wrestle control over the 8. The stubborn nature of the 8 would frustrate the 3's effort to be the controlling partner in the relationship. However, if both people are evolved souls the relationship can be deeply satisfying. The 3 Gua's deep-rooted, steady nature would mix well with the noble energy of the 8. Both tend to be organized and progressive thinkers, and *constructing* things together is the surest way of remaining close as a couple. Sexual union can be very intense, earthy and creative. *This couple belongs to opposite groups, one is East Life and the other is West Life.*

8 Gua with a 4 Gua
Elemental relationship: EARTH-WOOD

The 8 Gua with an 4 Gua indicate a natural tug a war with the 4 Gua trying to wrestle control over the 8. The stubborn nature of the 8 would frustrate the 4's effort to be the controlling partner in the relationship. However, if both people are evolved souls, the relationship can be deeply satisfying. The 4 Gua's malleable nature would mix well with the noble energy of the 8. The romantic nature of the 4 can win over, rather than control, the stable energy of the 8 Gua. Sexual union can be very intense, earthy and romantic. *This couple belongs to opposite groups, one is East Life and the other is West Life.*

8 Gua with a 6 Gua
Elemental relationship: EARTH-METAL

The 8 Gua matched with an 6 Gua is considered very compatible energy. The steady and noble energy of the 8 is a good compliment to the authoritative energy of the 6. This is heaven and earth energy, however at times the 6 Gua can slightly deplete the 8 who would be the supporter in the relationship. On a more negative note, un-evolved 8's can be hoarders, and the 6 can be self-absorbed—this would cause a great deal of conflict. If the souls were very developed and clear, the match can have heavenly aspects with both people leaning to things spiritual. Sexual union can be deep, earthy and extremely connected. *This couple both belong to the West Life Group.*

8 Gua with a 7 Gua
Elemental relationship: EARTH-METAL

The 8 Gua with an 7 Gua is excellent and considered very well-matched. The earthiness of the 8 grounds the nervous energy of the 7. The 7 brings the beauty and liveliness to the relationship, as the 8's can be more serious and stubborn. However, the 8 is considered the 'giver' in the relationship as the 7 does slightly deplete their energy. If the 8 is not developed they will lean towards greed, and the 7 will go to excesses and affairs. Sexual union can be highly sensuous, earthy and deeply gratifying for both parties. *This couple both belong to the West Life Group.*

8 Gua with an 8 Gua
Elemental relationship: EARTH-EARTH

The 8 Gua with another 8 Gua indicates friends and lovers. The noble and steadfast nature of the 8's can bring harmony and stability if the couple is developed. If not, head butting over how things should be done will occur with a digging in the heels and being implacable. Greed, hoarding and being remote will leave each other feeling deprived in the relationship. If the couple is higher in consciousness, each will bring out the nobleness, generosity and spirituality that is possible for these Guas. Sexual union can be very intense and earthy. *This couple both belong to the West Life Group.*

8 Gua with a 9 Gua
Elemental relationship: EARTH-FIRE

The 8 Gua with an 9 Gua is considered very well-matched with lots of potential. The 9 would be the 'giver' in the relationship supporting his/her spouse extremely well. They will fire up, fuel and support their mates with all that they have to offer—ideas, money and love. The 8 Gua will bring their stable, earth energy to the fiery, rasher nature of the 9. When these Guas are not very evolved the stubbornness of the 8 can totally irritate the 9's sharp intellect and superior attitude. Sexual union can be very intense, and these people can be very loyal and passionate lovers. *This couple belongs to opposite groups, one is East Life and the other is West Life.*

9 Gua in Romantic Relationships or Marriages

9 Gua with a 1 Gua
Elemental relationship: FIRE-WATER

The 1 Gua with a 9 Gua is oddly enough very compatible, often creating "steamy" love affairs and hot romance. However, the 1 Gua can completely put out the *fiery* nature of the 9 Gua if they are not in succinct or not grounded. If the souls are spiritually evolved, the high emotions/intellect of the 1 Gua will be well-received by the brilliant, fiery goddess energy of the 9's. Sexual union can be highly charged, sensuous and create a lot of *heat* that would be apparent even to casual onlookers. *This couple both belong to the East Life Group.*

9 Gua with a 2 Gua
Elemental relationship: FIRE-EARTH

The 2 Gua with a 9 Gua is a good match. The 2 Gua is really supported and fired up by the 9's energy. The 9 will enjoy the naturally calm nature of the 2 which perfectly complements the wild, fiery nature of the 9. These energies balance and feed each other beautifully. Sexual union can be hot, unconventional and exciting. *This couple belongs to opposite groups, one is East Life and the other is West Life.*

9 Gua with a 3 Gua
Elemental relationship: FIRE-WOOD

The 3 Gua with a 9 Gua are considered the "perfect match". The high-energy 3 Gua is a true supporter of the 9's fiery nature. The super intellect of the 9 and the progressive thinking 3's can be unstoppable. They are perfectly suited to capture whatever they are focused on as a couple—often this is fame for them both. If they are un-evolved, they can create a raging fire together and burn anyone in their path! Sexual union will be hot and intense. *This couple both belong to the East Life Group.*

9 Gua with a 4 Gua
Elemental relationship: FIRE-WOOD

The 4 Gua with a 9 Gua is a highly compatible match. The 4 Gua provides loyal support to the 9, making them the 'giver' in the relationship. The fiery intellect of the 9 Gua is an excellent match for the romantic and often scholarly 4. On the negative side, with the indecisive 4 and the rashness of the 9, sparks can fly. These two Guas are indicative of fame, and there could be some unhealthy competitiveness if the couple is not connected. The best way for a long marriage is the meeting of minds and hearts through clear communication. Sexual union can be intense and hot! *This couple both belong to the East Life Group.*

9 Gua with a 6 Gua
Elemental relationship: FIRE-METAL

In general, the match of a 6 Gua with a 9 Gua is not a compatible and could be difficult. Nevertheless, they will be attracted by their shared high intellect and thinking power. The 9's can totally 'melt' down the energy of the 6; naturally this will cause a conflict with the 6 whose nature is to rule and exert power. Sparks could fly, sharp words and hot debates over ideas could happen on a regular basis. However, if both people are advanced in consciousness, the union can be quite titillating and exciting with a spectacular exchange of ideas—a true power couple. Sexual union can be just as exciting with each succumbing to their passionate natures. *This couple belongs to opposite groups, one is East Life and the other is West Life.*

9 Gua with a 7 Gua
Elemental relationship: FIRE-METAL

In general, the 7 Gua matched up with a 9 Gua is considered extremely negative and ill-suited. The 9 may try to control their partner with their passionate opinions and ideas, and the 7 will rebel using their sharp tongues. If not sufficiently evolved, conflict could be a daily event. However, if they are advanced in consciousness, the relationship can be exciting on several levels—the intellect, sexual, and spiritual. Both the 9 and the 7 bring passion, beauty, sensuousness, and brilliant intellect. These Guas can be a powerful couple when the significant energy is directed to the greater good. Sexual union can be intense, beautiful and deeply sensual. *This couple belongs to opposite groups, one is East Life and the other is West Life.*

9 Gua with an 8 Gua
Elemental relationship: FIRE-EARTH

The 9 Gua with an 8 Gua is considered very well-matched with lots of potential. The 9 would be the 'giver' in the relationship supporting his/her spouse extremely well. They will fire up, fuel and support their mates with all that they have to offer—ideas, money and love. The 8 Gua will bring their stable, earth energy to the fiery, rasher nature of the 9. When these Guas are not very evolved the stubbornness of the 8 can totally irritate the 9's sharp intellect and superior attitude. Sexual union can be very intense, and these people can be very loyal and passionate lovers. *This couple belongs to opposite groups, one is East Life and the other is West Life.*

9 Gua with a 9 Gua
Elemental relationship: FIRE-FIRE

The match of the 9 Guas can be a something to behold, and generally it is considered to be a good match. The energy of this couple has the potential to be great, each bringing out the best in each other, or disaster. The 9's who are not developed can exhibit paranoia, rashness and very aggressive behavior. These people can start revolutions and stir up trouble. When they are advanced in consciousness however, they can have a powerful influence on people with their noble and wise ideas and deliver them with passion. Sexual union can be *fiery* in capital letters! *This couple both belong to the East Life Group.*

CHAPTER SEVEN
Workplace and Career

Life Guas and Working Relationships

The Eight Mansions system provides lots of information regarding the relationships you have with co-workers and management. If you wish to better understand these bonds, learn their Life-Gua number and then refer to the Eight Mansion chart on page 12. You must know their full birthday—month, day, and year. Based primarily on the five-element theory, the following information offers some guidelines and suggestions. Each Gua has a particular energy that influences a person's propensities and personality traits, which are listed below. Also include their animal year of birth.

WATER Energy: 1 Guas

If you are a 1 Gua, the best employees for you to hire, to work with or have as a business partner are 9, 3, 4, 6, 7, and another 1 like yourself. You may feel as if you've found a kindred spirit in a 1 Gua. You will have a great deal of control and influence over a 9 Gua. This person will also make a good business partner if you want the lead position or controlling interest. 3 and 4 Guas are highly compatible with you but may weaken your energy at times, while 6 and 7 Guas have an energy that will support of you. The 2 and 8 Guas can control your energy and this may be your boss's Gua number.

Pay attention to the six animal clashes. For example, you may be the same Life Gua (1) as your business partner but you are a 1 Pig and he/she is 1 Snake.

Employees	Partners	Boss	Companions
Water, wood or metal	Fire	Earth	Water or wood
1, 3, 4, 6, 7	9	2, 8	1, 3, 4

The Six Animal Clashes	
Rat	Horse
Ox	Goat
Tiger	Monkey
Rabbit	Rooster
Dragon	Dog
Snake	Pig

EARTH Energy: 2 and 8 Guas

If you are a 2 or 8 Gua, the best employees for you to hire, to work with or have as a business partner are 1, 2, 9, 6, 7, or an 8. You may become friends with an 8 or a 2 Gua. You will have a great deal of influence over a 1 Gua, so if you want controlling interest in a partnership, this is the person with whom to team up with. A 6 or a 7 Gua will slightly deplete your energy. Meanwhile, a 3 or a 4 Gua will try to control you and this may be your boss's Gua number. A 9 Gua will invigorate you and support your ideas and position.

Pay attention to the six animal clashes. For example, you may be the same Life Gua (2) as your business partner but you are a 2 Rabbit and he/she is 2 Rooster.

Employees	Partners	Boss	Companions
Water, Earth, Metal, Fire	Water	Wood	Earth, Fire
1, 2, 6, 7, 8, 9	1	3, 4	2, 8, 9

The Six Animal Clashes	
Rat	Horse
Ox	Goat
Tiger	Monkey
Rabbit	Rooster
Dragon	Dog
Snake	Pig

WOOD Energy: 3 and 4 Guas

If you are a 3 or 4 Gua, the best employees for you to hire, to work with or have as a business partner are 1, 3, 4, 2, and 8. You may be close friends with 3 and 4 Gua employees. You will have a great deal of control over a 2 or an 8 Gua, these people are also the best to team up with if you want to run the show. A 1 Gua will best support you. A 9 Gua will try to control you. They may also drain your energy altogether, leaving you feeling exhausted most of the time—this may also be your boss's Gua number.

Pay attention to the six animal clashes. For example, you may be the same Life Gua (3 or 4) as your business partner but you are a 3 Goat and he/she is 3 Ox.

Employees	Partners	Boss	Companions
Water, Earth, Wood	Fire	Metal	Water or wood
1, 2, 3, 4, 8	9	6, 7	1, 3, 4,

The Six Animal Clashes	
Rat	Horse
Ox	Goat
Tiger	Monkey
Rabbit	Rooster
Dragon	Dog
Snake	Pig

FIRE Energy: 9 Guas

If you are a 9 Gua, the best employees for you to hire, to work with or have as a business partner are 3, 4, 6, 7, and 9. You may enjoy the company of other 9 Guas, especially on an intellectual level. You will have control over 6 and 7 Guas and can stop them cold in their tracks! Choose either Gua if you want supremacy in a business relationship. You are compatible with 3 and 4 Guas, who can be your greatest champion. But 8 and 2 Guas will deplete your energy. A 1 Gua will totally wash you out, try to control you, and dampen your spirits and ideas; this may be your boss.

Pay attention to the six animal clashes. For example, you may be the same Life Gua (9) as your business partner but you are a 9 Dog and he/she is a 9 Dragon.

Employees	Partners	Boss	Companions
Wood, Metal, Fire	Metal	Wood	Wood, Fire
3, 4, 6, 7, 9	6, 7	1	3, 4, 9

The Six Animal Clashes	
Rat	Horse
Ox	Goat
Tiger	Monkey
Rabbit	Rooster
Dragon	Dog
Snake	Pig

METAL Energy: 6 and 7 Guas

If you are a 6 or 7 Gua, the best employees for you to hire, to work with or have as a business partner are 2, 8, 3, 4 and 1. Don't be surprised if you bond or collaborate with another 6 or 7. You will wield a good amount of control and influence over a 3 or 4, so choose this type of person if you want the upper hand in business. A 1 Gua is extremely compatible and supportive and will help you turn your idea into reality. 9 Guas can melt you down and totally wipe out your energy; he or she is probably your superior at work.

Pay attention to the six animal clashes. For example, you may be the same Life Gua (6 or 7) as your business partner but you are a 7 Rabbit and he/she is a 7 Rooster.

Employees	Partners	Boss	Companions
Earth, Wood, Water	Wood	Fire	Metal, Water
2, 8, 3, 4, 1	3, 4	9	6, 7, 1

The Six Animal Clashes	
Rat	Horse
Ox	Goat
Tiger	Monkey
Rabbit	Rooster
Dragon	Dog
Snake	Pig

For those of you who spend a great deal of time in an office environment, this information can be invaluable. Most managers have no choice; they must be present to help run the company and deal with employees. So, hiring supervisory staff with this knowledge in mind will create energy that works for you. It's much better than spending tortuous days at the office, navigating conflicting personalities.

Face Your Power Direction

In Feng Shui, direction is everything; this is how energy comes to you and supports you. So if you haven't discovered your Life-Gua number using the Eight Mansions chart on page 12, do so now. Remember, in this system you have four good directions relating to different areas of your life—one for money, one for health luck, another for relationship luck, and finally a direction for stability.

Sheng Chi (+90) is your power direction and specifically applies to money-luck, power, and authority. You will want to face this direction while sitting at your desk to experience the best wealth and career-luck possible. If you are unable to activate this direction, use your +80 direction which supports health and wealth, as an alternate.

If you work at your computer a great deal, place your monitor and keyboard so that you may face towards your Sheng Chi. Same goes if the phone is your mainstay, always face your Sheng Chi while you're doing business on it to enjoy maximum influence over your clients, customers, employees, and so forth.

If you spend an equal amount of time on the computer and on the phone, face your +90 and +80 directions. This is what is meant by activating a direction—using it, facing it. If you are permitted to install a gorgeous wall fountain, you will have a great office space.

When consulting directly with a company, I generally reserve the +90 (Sheng Chi) direction for top executives, and I will situate subordinates in good directions that do not compete with upper management. It is best to place employees in their +70 (Yen Nien) direction, which is auspicious for relationships and harmony in the workplace. If you are lucky enough to have this information, you definitely have an advantage. Simply take a compass direction using your SmartPhone. There are some very good apps that are very accurate that are based on Global Positioning System (GPS).

Life Gua Number	Power Directions	
	Power (+90)	2nd Power (+80)
1	Southeast	East
2	Northeast	West
3	South	North
4	North	South
6	West	Northeast
7	Northwest	Southwest
8	Southwest	Northwest
9	East	Southeast

The Emperor's Position is to secure success and power for the CEO or President of a business. He or she should be placed in the far, upper left-hand corner of the office layout or floor plan. If another person is placed there, it may invite fierce rivalry and competition.

By now you are aware of, not only of your Life-Gua number, but whether you are East Life Group or West Life Group. Remember, according to the Eight Mansions formula, every person in the world is born with four auspicious directions and four harmful directions. These directions will attract a slightly different kind of luck to you. To enhance career and money, the best directions to use are your +90 (*Sheng Chi*), +80 (*Tien Yi*), and the +70 (*Yen Nien*). They represent your wealth/power, unexpected wealth from heaven, and great connections/relationships respectively.

The Emperor's Position

Every person within an organization can benefit from Feng Shui to improve their personal career-luck by simply re-orientating the sitting direction alone. However, it is the CEO's office and sitting direction which will have the greatest impact on the success or failure of the business. For executives, the office located furthest from the entrance is the most commanding space; it is the position of power. This is known as the *Emperor's Position* because it offers the most protection from unwelcomed intruders and should be reserved for the head of the company. If this office is held by a female, it is known as the Empresses' Position. In ancient times, the Emperor was placed some distance from the main entrance, and visitors would have to go through an army of soldiers to reach him.

If another member of the management team resides in this location, there will be fierce competition with the CEO causing rivalry and discord. I consulted with a cutting-edge software firm in Houston, Texas who had this scenario. Once I reminded them to switch the CEO/President to the 'Emperor's Position', everything calmed down. Not only that, this start-up company received numerous, rich investors for their projects. When Feng Shui is implemented considering the entire chain of command within the organizational structure, then the potential for good fortune is considerably enhanced.

For extra luck, always enter the office building via one of your four auspicious directions (+90, +80, +70 or +60). That way even before you even begin work, you'll be energizing good fortunes.

CHAPTER EIGHT
Applications for Home and Office

Eight Mansions has several practical applications. In this chapter we'll learn how to apply it to your home or office.

Now that you know your Life-Gua number, you'll be able to improve the Feng Shui of your home and business environments considerably, thereby maximizing the potential of the rooms in which you live and work. You will need to either locate or draw a simple floor plan of your home or office to make changes. Later in this chapter, you will see examples of how to divide up your floor plan and superimpose the Eight Mansions values (+90, -70, +60 and so forth) plus the directions.

On the next page, you'll see how Eight Mansions is actually applied. All of these principles are discussed one by one and in detail in this chapter. You will want to take a compass direction of your home or office (page 231). Then have a simple sketch of your floor to make notes on how to arrange things. For an office the desk direction is the most important. A good door to enter the building is essential.

The Doors Always use a door that faces one of best directions (+60, +70, +80, and +90) door 90% of the time.	
The Beds The headboard should be towards one of your good directions. Select a direction that supports what you want, romance, wealth or good health (+70, +80, and +90).	
The Kitchen and Stove Stoves are best located in one of your bad/negative direction (-90, -80, -70, or -60). Stoves 'burn up' bad luck.	
Sit or Face While sitting at your desk working, giving a presentation, negotiating a deal, making a sale over the phone, giving a speech or meeting someone, face one of your good directions to support you (+60, +70, +80, and +90).	
The Toilets The toilets in the house should be located on your bad directions (-60, -70, -80 and -90).	

Use Good Doors!

Your main door of use rates #1 in Classical Feng Shui. Whether that is a front door or an internal garage door; it must activate good energy. In addition to your four good directions, there are several more, based on Advanced Eight Mansions that are also excellent. See the next page.

If your Gua Number is...	......and your main door is facing:
1	South, you should have excellent relationships. East, great health and Southeast superior money-luck.
2	Northwest, harmonious household. Northeast or West, get high position and riches.
3	Southeast lots of children, and promotions. South or North, you get riches and vitality.
4	East, your family will produce brilliant scholars. South or North, fame and riches that last.
6	Southwest, you'll be prosperous and good family life. Northeast or West, you and children will be wildly successful.
7	Northeast, good and successful family life. Northwest or Southwest, good stability, and wealth grows.
8	West, good relationships and children. Southwest or Northwest, the house is filled with riches.
9	North, plenty of gold and silver for the family. East or Southeast, you will good children and intelligent children.

Good and bad doors for EAST Life Groups

(based on Eight Mansions and Advanced Eight Mansions)

East Life Group (1, 3, 4 and 9 Guas)			
Good Doors to Use:	**Exact Degrees**	**Bad Doors to Use:**	**Exact Degrees**
North	337° to 22°	**Southwest** 2	217° to 232°
South	157° to 202°	**West** 2	262° to 277°
East	67° to 112°	**Northwest** 2	307° to 322°
Southeast	112° to 157°	**Northeast** 1	22° to 37°
Northeast 3	52° to 67°	**Northeast** 2	37° to 52°
Southwest 1	202° to 217°		
Southwest 3	232° to 247°		
West 1	247° to 262°		
West 3	277° to 292°		
Northwest 1	292° to 307°		
Northwest 3	322° to 337°		

Good and bad doors for WEST Life Groups

(based on Eight Mansions and Advanced Eight Mansions)

West Life Group (2, 6, 7 and 8 Guas)			
Good Doors to Use:	**Exact Degrees**	**Bad Doors to Use:**	**Exact Degrees**
Southwest	202° to 247°	**North** 1, 2, 3	337° to 22°
West	247° to 292°	**East** 2	82° to 97°
Northwest	292° to 337°	**Southeast** 1	112° to 127°
Northeast	22° to 67°	**Southeast** 2	127° to 142°
East 1	67° to 82°	**South** 2	172° to 187°
East 3	97° to 112°		
Southeast 3	142° to 157°		
South 1	157° to 172°		
South 3	187° to 202°		

Bed Direction

Bedrooms are such an important part of our life as we spend 1/3 of our lives in the sleep state. Therefore, the energy should be conducive to harmonious living. Since the master bedroom is crucial, particular attention should be paid to this room as it will determine the luck of the patriarch, head of household or breadwinner (male or female).

This room governs the finances, harmony and well-being of the family. It will determine the relationship luck, personal and business. The woman of the house's luck is also affected by the master bedroom location and arrangement.

Feng Shui places great emphasis on, not only the location of the bedroom, but the bed direction as well. The sleeping direction is of vital significance for both married and single people. This area of the house is an opportunity not to be missed to enhance your life.

The Stove & Kitchen

According to the old texts on the Eight Mansion formula, the placement and orientation of the stove and kitchen is one of the most potent of all. This formula requires that kitchens be assigned to your negative or unlucky sectors. The premise behind this important idea is that the fire will *'burn up'* your bad luck thus attracting auspicious, good luck and events. This also applies to stove locations—they should be placed in one of your negative sectors/directions (-90, -80, -70, or -60).

Eight Mansions Kitchen and Stove Locations

If the STOVE is located in your:	*This will result in:*
+90 Money (Sheng Chi)	Women can't conceive, miscarriages, unpopularity, foolish children if conceived, no livelihood/career or money.
+80 Health (Tien Yi)	Much sickness in the household, contracting a serious disease, difficulty in getting well and no harmony in the house.
+70 Relationships (Yen Nein)	Lots of quarrels, difficulty in getting married or finding a life partner, bad affairs, and a short life.
+60 Stability (Gu Wei)	A short life, no money-luck, and always being poor.
-60 Set-Backs (Wo Hai)	Suppress this sector with a stove and there will be very little sickness in the household.
-70 Lawsuits and Affairs (Wu Gwei)	There will be no fires, sickness, and no money problems. Good employer and support. No affairs or lawsuits.
-80 Bad Health and Betrayals (Lui Sha)	Can have money, children, and no lawsuits. No disasters and excellent health.
-90 Divorce (Cheuh Ming)	Long life, good health, lots of money and children.

The Toilets

This is for examination purposes; you can't move a toilet once the home is built. You do have a choice if you are building or selecting a new one. Toilets should be located in negative areas of the house (-90, -80, -70, or -60). If your master bathroom/toilet is located in one of your good areas, find another toilet to frequent. The bath/shower sinks and closets are not a problem, but a toilet is if it is located in one of your auspicious locations (+90, +80, +70, or +60). Having and using toilets in your good locations can destroy specific types of luck represented by the location, they are as follows:

- Toilets located in your +90 will cause struggles with money
- Toilets located in your +80 will harm your health
- Toilets located in your +70 may lead to 'crappy' romance-luck and relationships

Desk Direction

Today, more and more people work from home. The more hours you are working at your desk, the more important the facing direction is. Ideally you should face your +90 if you have a home-based business.

Equally important would be to face good directions (+90, +80, +70 or +60) while negotiating, giving a presentation, or making a speech—all of these actions affect our luck and energy. So make sure that your desk and chair are positioned to capture one of your most auspicious directions.

Floor Plan and Application

In this example, the homeowner is a 9 Life Gua and the house faces East. The front door is excellent (+90), the interior garage is not as good which is angled to the Northeast. The owner's bed should be place on the South or North wall. The stove is located on the North and may harm relationships/romance. The toilets are in the NW and South (acceptable). While sitting at the desk, he/she should face East.

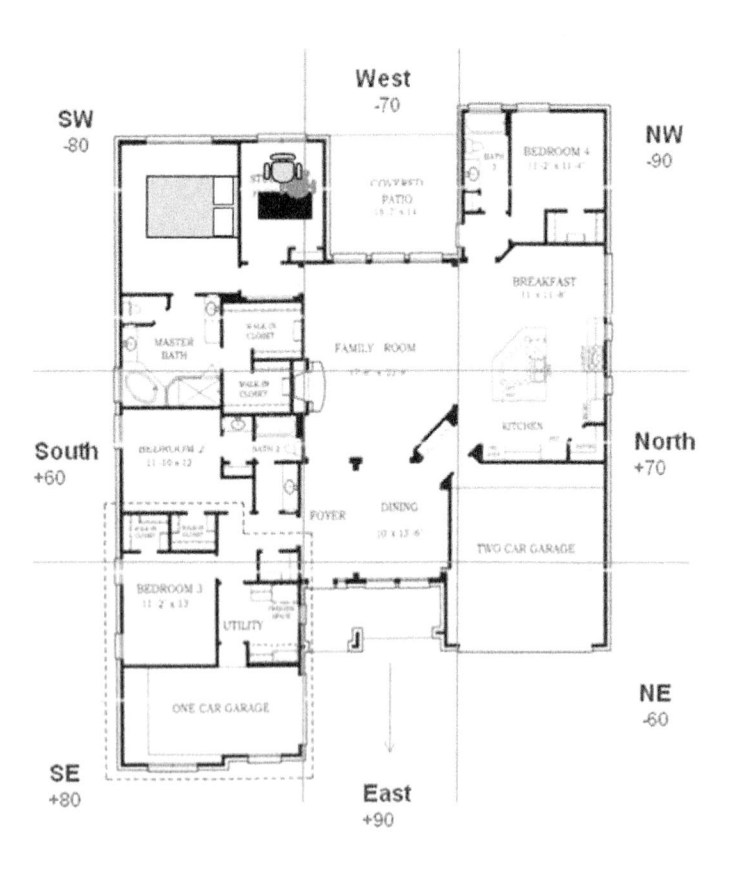

Eight Mansions Zodiac Feng Shui

Location and Direction

There is a big difference between direction and location, Eight Mansions makes use of both. See the examples below and arrange your home accordingly.

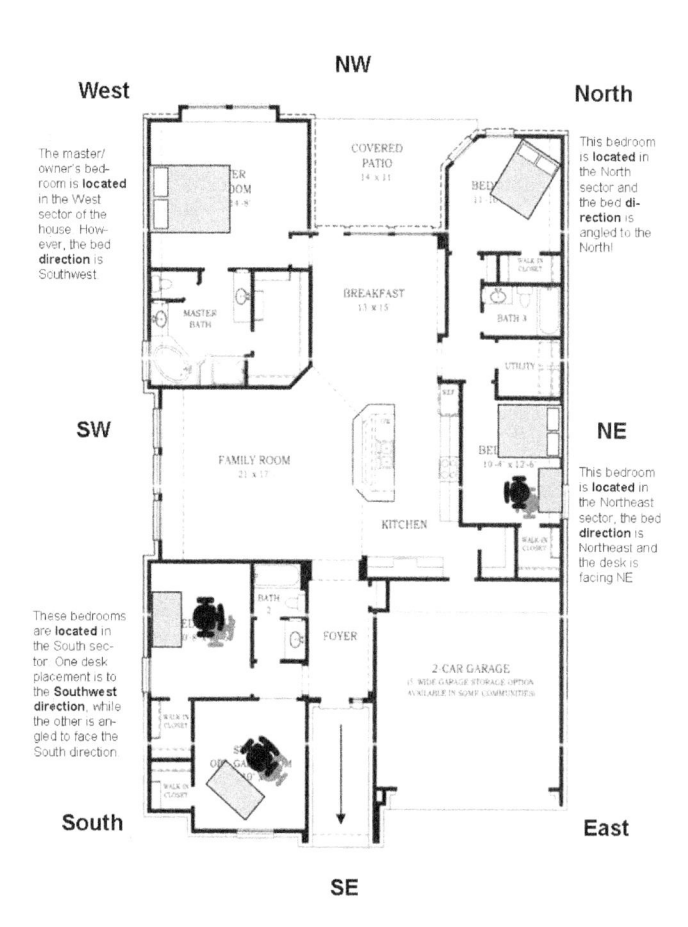

NW

West

The master/owner's bedroom is **located** in the West sector of the house. However, the bed **direction** is Southwest.

North

This bedroom is **located** in the North sector and the bed **direction** is angled to the North!

SW

NE

This bedroom is **located** in the Northeast sector, the bed **direction** is Northeast and the desk is facing NE.

These bedrooms are **located** in the South sector. One desk placement is to the **Southwest direction**, while the other is angled to face the South direction.

South

East

SE

Summary & the Three Hits!

There are many layers to Feng Shui. Moving a few things around in your home or office can be very, very effective! Before entering into romantic relationships, refer to the information presented in this book. Business relationships can also have long-term effects on your life and money, so use Feng Shui to get a good advantage.

The Eight Mansions system is a simple and powerful way to do this. Often people have a particular area of their life that they want to change; relationships, health or wealth. To truly affect a category, you will need at least *three hits*. For example the bedroom may be located in your +70, AND your bed direction is also to your +70 direction. You would enter a door that is your +70. Your stove or toilet would be located in your -70. Your desk would face your +70. That's a total of 5 hits! Or you want more prosperity. Face your +90 while sitting at your desk. Enter the house from a +90 door. Place your bed to your +90 direction. The stove or toilet could be located on your -90. Or you could mix it up and tackle all three categories of Feng Shui.

Here's a review; beds, desks, doors should activate your +90, +80, +70 or +60 directions. Stove and toilets should be in your -90, -80, -70 or -60 directions or locations. See page 205.

For the best luck in these categories

Relationships: use the +70, -70 and -80.
Wealth: use the +90, +80, -90, and -80.
Health: use the +80 and -80.

Glossary of Terms

This book includes Feng Shui terms using both Wade-Giles and Pinyin; in several instances the glossary gives both spellings. The Chinese-to-English translations also include some in Mandarin and others in Cantonese; I've chosen the ones most used by my teacher, Grandmaster Yap Cheng Hai and their spellings.

auspicious: The Chinese favor the term *auspicious*, meaning something is lucky, and good events will ensue.

Ba Gua: Also spelled as Pa Kua; an octagonal arrangement of the eight trigrams or Guas.

BaZhai: the Eight Mansion system, also spelled PaChai. This system is also known as the East-West System and Eight House Feng Shui.

Big Dipper Casting Golden Light: Known as *Jin Guang Dou Lin Jing* in Chinese and also spelled as *Kam Kwong Dou Lam King*. This style of Eight Mansions is used in this book; it is also called *Golden Star Classic*.

Black Hat Sect: A new school of Feng Shui invented in the 1980s. It was brought to the Western world by Professor Thomas Lin Yun, a Buddhist monk of the Black Hat Order of Tibetan Buddhism. Although not considered an authentic system of Feng Shui, Black Hat is the most recognized style in the world except in Asian countries, which are most familiar with traditional schools of Feng Shui.

Book of Changes: Also known as the *I Ching*.

Buddhism: is a nontheistic *(not having a belief in a god)* religion that encompasses a variety of traditions, beliefs and practices largely based on teachings attributed to Siddhartha Gautama, who is commonly known as the Buddha, meaning "the awakened one". According to Buddhist tradition, the Buddha lived and taught in the eastern part of the Indian subcontinent sometime between the 6th and 4th centuries BCE.

cardinal directions: Points of geographic orientation—North, South, East and West. The specific and exact points of these directions are 0/360, North; 90 degrees, East; 180 degrees, South; and 270 degrees, West.

Chai: House, also spelled Zhai.

Chen: One of the eight trigrams of the Ba Gua. It represents the eldest son, thunder and spring. In the Later Heaven arrangement of the Ba Gua, the Chen trigram is located in the East.

Chueh Ming: In the Eight Mansions system, this represents total loss, divorce and bankruptcy. According to Master Yap's numeric representation, it is the -90.

Chi: The vital life-force energy of the universe and everything in it; sometimes chi is referred to as *cosmic breath*. It is also spelled *ch'i* or *qi* and is pronounced *chee*.

Chien: One of the eight trigrams of the Ba Gua also spelled as *Qian*. It represents the father, the heavens, and late autumn. In the Later Heaven arrangement of the Ba Gua, the Chien trigram is located in the Northwest.

Chinese Lunar and Solar Calendars: All Feng Shui experts worth their salt use the Chinese Solar Calendar as the basis of their practice as its formulas are very time sensitive and this calendar is very accurate. This is not to say they don't celebrate the Lunar New Year, in fact, they do; the *Chinese New Year*, as well as other holidays, is extremely important. The ancient Chinese used the Solstices and Equinoxes to fix their calendar. 15º Aquarius is exactly half way between the Winter Solstice and the Spring Equinox (on the Northern Hemisphere). In the past, Chinese Lunar New Year started around the Winter Solstice. In 104 BC Emperor Han Wu Di moved the beginning of the year so that the Winter Solstice occurs in the eleventh month. Winter Solstice falls on the 15th day of Zi/Rat month, the middle of the winter, 15° Aquarius is the Sun's position. Whenever the sun reaches that position that is the Chinese Solar New Year. This could be February 3, 4, 5. The Chinese chose the 15º Aquarius as the starting point of the Spring season and the New Year. The Spring Equinox falls exactly in the middle of the Spring season; this is always on the 15th day of Mao/Rabbit month. Lunar calendar defines the lunar month on the first day of the appearance of the New Moon. A Lunar New Year begins on the 1st day of this new "moon". A lunar month is from the new moon to the next new moon. The ecliptic was divided into 12 equal divisions by the ancients. The Chinese Solar year is based on these 24 divisions called 24 solar terms. The year is divided into 24 periods of 15 days. Li Chun is the first of the 24 terms. The names of these divisions date back to the late Chou Dynasty (10450—221BC). The most important of the 24 terms is the New Year.

Chinese Zodiac: is a system that relates each year to an animal and its reputed attributes, according to a 12-year mathematical cycle. It remains popular in several East Asian countries, such as China, Vietnam, Korea and Japan.

Classical Feng Shui: Also known as Traditional Feng Shui. It is the authentic, genuine Feng Shui that has been developed and applied for hundreds, even thousands, of years in Asia. Sophisticated forms are practiced in Hong Kong, Taiwan, Malaysia, and Singapore. Classical Feng Shui is just being introduced and practiced in Western countries, and has not reached main stream status. The traditional systems of Feng Shui are the *San He*, meaning three combinations, and *San Yuan* or three cycles. All techniques, methods, and formulas will be under one or the other. Feng Shui masters and practitioners will use both systems as one comprehensive body of knowledge.

compass, Chinese: See Luo Pan.

Cosmic Trinity: Known in Chinese as *Tien-Di-Ren*. Three categories of luck, specifically heaven-luck, man-luck, and earth-luck. The Chinese believe heaven-luck is fixed, however, humans have control over Feng Shui (earth-luck) and personal effort (man-luck).

Dao: also spelled *Tao*, is a Chinese concept signifying the way, path, route, or sometimes known as the doctrine or principle. Within the context of traditional Chinese philosophy and religion, Tao is a metaphysical concept originating with Lao Tzu that gave rise to a religion and philosophy (Taoism). The concept of Tao was shared with Confucianism and Zen Buddhism. Within these contexts Tao signifies the primordial essence or fundamental nature of the universe. In Taoism, Chinese Buddhism and Confucianism, the object of spiritual practice is to *become one with the Tao* or to harmonize one's will with Nature in order to achieve effortless action; this involves meditative and moral practices.

direction: One of the most important aspects of determining the energy of a site or structure is

dragon: In Feng Shui a dragon is a mountain. Dragon is a term also used for something powerful or curving, as in the mythical body of a dragon. It can apply to land and water. The Chinese so revere the dragon that it is used in multiple applications and meanings.

Early Heaven Ba Gua: This is the first arrangement of the eight trigrams; known as the *Ho Tien* or *Fu Xi* Ba Gua in Chinese. It can be easily recognized as the Chien trigram (three solid lines) and is always placed on the top. This is the arrangement used in Ba Gua mirrors to deter sha Chi.

Earth Luck: One of the three categories of luck that humans can experience; your luck will increase by using Feng Shui, also known as Earth Luck. The Chinese word for earth is *Di*.

East Life Group: In the Eight Mansions system, people are divided into the East or West group. The 1, 3, 4 and 9 Life Guas are part of the East Life Group.

Eight House: This is another name for the Eight Mansions; in Chinese it is *Pa Chai* or *BaZhai*.

Eight House Bright Mirror: In Chinese *Pa Chai Ming Jing*, is one of the eight different styles of the Eight Mansions system. This style uses the sitting direction of the house instead of the facing.

Eight Life Aspirations: Also known as the *Eight Life Stations*, these stations correspond to a point on the Ba Gua and an aspect of life—South, fame; Southwest, marriage; Southeast, wealth; North, career; and so forth. This is the work of Black Hat Sect founder Lin Yun. Eight Life Stations is not found in classic texts or part of the genuine Feng Shui of ancient practice and principles. It is neither an aspect of the Eight Mansions system nor even a derivative of that system. Some popular Feng Shui books that promote Classical Feng Shui also include the Eight Life Aspirations, which only adds to the confusion.

Eight Mansions: also known as *Eight House Feng Shui*, the

East-West System, *BaZhai* which is also spelled *PaChai;* this system, based on your personal Gua/Kua Number, gives you the four good and four bad directions to use and mitigate in your living space or wherever you happen to be such as at a meeting, your offices, a seminar and so forth to bring good fortune.

Eight Wandering Stars: also known as the *Big Wandering Sky*, these stars are matched with the nine stars of the Big Dipper, they are as follows: Tan Lang (*Greedy Wolf* aka *Ravenous Wolf*) is matched with **Sheng Chi**; Jue Men *(Huge Door* aka *Great Door)* is matched with **Tien Yi**; Wu Chu *(Military Arts)* is matched with **Yen Nien**; Tso Fu & Fu Pi *(Left/Right Assistant* aka the *Big Dipper's Handle*) is matched with **Fu Wei**; Lu Chun *(Rewards/Salary)* is matched with **Wo Hai;** Lien Zheng *(Five Ghosts aka Chastity)* is matched with **Wu Gwei**; Wen Qu *(Literary Arts* aka *The Scholar)* is matched with **Lui Sha**; Tien Kong *(Broken Soldier* aka *Destructive Army)* is matched with **Cheuh Ming**. These nine stars and their unique energy are very important in many Feng Shui systems. More on the nine stars in Chapter Five; the Chinese names above are also the 'secret names' of the nine stars.

energy: The Chinese call energy chi (also spelled *qi*) and pronounced ***chee***. Our entire universe is energy; there are many types of chi—human, environmental, and heaven (the solar system).

esoteric: Knowledge that is available only to a narrow circle of enlightened or initiated people or a specially educated group. Feng Shui is part of Chinese metaphysics and is considered esoteric.

external environment: This covers the terrain and topography, including mountains, water, and other natural formations. It also encompasses man-made features, such as roads, pools, retaining walls, highways, poles, drains, washes, tall buildings, stop signs, fire hydrants, and other structures.

facing direction: The front side of the home or building, generally where the front or main door is located and faces the street.

Feng: The Chinese word for **wind;** pronounced *fung,* although *foong* is a more accurate sound.

Feng Shui: Known as *Kan Yu* (translated as *the way of heaven and earth*) until about a hundred years ago, the Chinese system of maximizing the accumulation of beneficial chi improves the quality of life and luck of the occupants of a particular building or location. The literal translation is wind and water; however, in Classical Feng Shui wind means *direction* and water means *energy*. Pronounced *foong shway.*

Feng Shui master: One who has mastered the skills of Classical Feng Shui and/or has been declared as such by his or her teacher, or both. Most Feng Shui masters from classic traditions will belong to a lineage of their teachers. This is also known as *a lineage carrier,* meaning the master carries on the teachings and practices of his or her education. A Feng Shui master generally oversees his or her own school and students, too.

Feng Shui schools: There are two major schools or branches (not physical locations, rather they are systems) of Classical Feng Shui, San He and San Yuan; hundreds of formulas, techniques, and systems serve as sub sets of either school. If you practice Classical Feng Shui, you use the San He and the San Yuan systems as one extensive body of knowledge. See the article in the compendium for details on each school.

Flying Stars: Known as *Xuan Kong Fei Xing* in Chinese, which means *mysterious void* or the *subtle mysteries of time and space.* It is a popular Feng Shui system that is superior in addressing the time aspect of energy. Refer to Chapter Four for additional information on this vast system.

Fu Wie: The direction and location for stability as it applies to the Eight Mansions system. According to Master Yap's numeric representation, it is the +60.

Fu Xi: A sage, king and shaman who was responsible for discovering and arranging the Early Heaven Ba Gua.

Gen: One of the eight trigrams of the Ba Gua also spelled as *Ken*. It represents the youngest son, the mountain and early spring. In the Later Heaven arrangement of the Ba Gua, the Gen trigram is located in the Northeast.

grandmaster of Feng Shui: This person has been practicing and teaching for many years, belongs to a respected lineage of masters, and has at least one master among his or her pupils.

Grandmaster Yap Cheng Hai (GMY): Master Yap was born and raised in Singapore; although he did live briefly in Xiamen, China for four years. He moved to Kuala Lumpur, Malaysia in 1963 to manage his uncle's business and soon became a citizen. Although his life was full, he pursued two passions, that of Feng Shui and Martial Arts. He began practicing Feng Shui professionally in the early 60's. He has consulted with prominent figures such as members of royalty, ministers, corporations, banks, and developers. His loyal client since the sixties, Paramount Garden consulted him to plan their townships that included SEA Park, Damansara Utama and Bandar Utama. GMY is quite famous in Southeast Asia for his *Water Dragon* techniques. He learned this specialized method from Grandmaster Chan Chuan Huai in Taiwan who created several billionaires there. GMY began teaching in the late 1990's to those wishing to learn authentic, Classical Feng Shui. I graduated from his 2001 class as a Master right after 9/11.

Gua: Alternatively spelled *Kua* and also known as a trigram. It represents one of eight Guas of the Ba Gua, defined by a combination of three solid or broken lines.

Gua Number: Also referred to as *Ming Gua* (nothing to do with the Ming Dynasty). To determine your personal Life Gua number, use your birthday. See Chapter Three for specific instructions.

GYM Code: this is a code devised by Grandmaster Yap to easily identify your good and bad directions in the Eight Mansions system; the +90, +80, +70, +60 are your *good* directions representing wealth, health, relationships/longevity and stability respectively. The code of -90, -80, -70, and -60 represent your *bad* directions that if activated, will cause divorce/bankruptcy, bad health/betrayals, affairs/lawsuits and setbacks respectively.

Heaven Luck: One of the three categories of luck that humans can experience. The Chinese believe every human has a destiny and a fate determined by the heavens (tien).

This category cannot be changed and is considered *fixed*. See also Tien-Di-Ren.

high-rise building: In the external environment, high-rise buildings and skyscrapers function as *virtual* or *urban mountains*.

Ho: The Chinese word for fire.

Ho Hai: Also known as *Wo Hai*. Part of the Eight Mansions system and can bring mishaps—nothing goes smoothly. According to Master Yap's numeric representation, this is the -60.

Hsia: pronounced *she-ah*; this is the name for the Chinese Solar Calendar based on the cycles of the Sun. The Solar Calendar regulates agriculture because the *Sun* determines the seasons; also used in all Feng Shui techniques for its accuracy. The solar year begins on February 4th or 5th, there are two possible dates is not because an uncertainly, but due to the fact that the Western calendar 'wobbles' because of the insertion of the extra day during 'leap years'.

Inauspicious: means very unlucky and in Feng Shui could indicate negative events.

I Ching: A philosophical and divinatory book based on the sixty-four hexagrams of Taoist mysticism. It is also known as the *Classic of Changes* or *Book of Changes*.

interior environment: The interior environment encompasses anything that falls within the walls of a structure, including kitchen, staircase, Master Bedroom + Family, fireplaces, bathrooms, hallways, dining room, bedrooms, appliances, furniture, and so on.

intercardinal directions: Northwest, Southwest, Northeast and Southeast.

Kan: One of the eight trigrams. It represents the middle son, the moon and mid-winter. In the Later Heaven Arrangement of the Ba Gua, it is located in the North.

Kun: One of the eight trigrams. It represents the mother, the earth and late summer. In the Later Heaven Arrangement of the Ba Gua, it is located in the Southwest.

Later Heaven Ba Gua: The second arrangement of the trigrams known as the *Wen Wang* or *Xien Tien* Ba Gua. This is used extensively in the application of Classical Feng Shui.

Li: One of the eight trigrams. It represents the middle daughter, fire and full summer. In the Later Heaven Arrangement of the Ba Gua, it is located in the South.

Life Gua Number: a number assigned to people, based on birthday and gender, in the Eight Mansions system (BaZhai also spelled Pa Chai).

Life-Gua Personalities™: a description of personality types based on the Life Gua number in the Eight Mansion system expanded on and trademarked by the author and first seen in *Classical Feng Shui for Wealth and Abundance.*

Life-Gua Zodiac Personalities™: this is an expanded version of the *Life Gua Personalities* which include the Zodiac animal year of birth.

Liu Sha: In the Eight Mansions system, it also known as the *Six Killings* direction and can bring backstabbing, affairs, and lawsuits. According to Master Yap's numeric representation, it is the -80.

location: A particular place or position, differing from the concept of *direction*. For example, your living room might be located on the South side of your home (location), but your desk faces North (direction).

lunar calendar: A calendar based on the cycles of the moon.

Lung: The Chinese word for dragon.

Luo Pan: The Luo Pan is the quintessential tool of a Feng Shui practitioner. It is a compass that contains four to forty concentric rings of information. The most popular model is approximately ten inches across, square, and often constructed of fine woods. The circle part of the Luo Pan is made of brass and rotates to align with the compass itself, which is located in the center. There are three major types of Luo Pans—the *San Yuan* Luo Pan, the *San He* Luo Pan, and the *Chung He* Luo Pan (also known as *Zong He* or *Zhung He*), which is a combination of the first two. Though Luo Pans have similar basic components, Feng Shui masters do customize their own with secret information for them and their students.

Luo Shu: A square that contains nine palaces or cells with a number in each; it adds to fifteen in any direction. The Luo Shu is also known as the *Magic Square of 15*.

Magic Life-Gua: some masters call your personal Gua number by many names—Magic Life-Gua, Ming Gua, or Life Gua.

main door: This is usually the front door of the home or business. If the occupants always enter the residence from the garage, this may also be considered a main door.

Man Luck: One of the three categories of luck that a human can experience. This area of fortune is mutable and defined by individual effort, such as hard work, study, education, experience, and good deeds. The Chinese word for man is *Ren*. See Tien-Di-Ren.

Ming Dynasty: A ruling dynasty of China, which lasted from 1368 to 1644.

Ming Gua: another name for Life-Gua.

Nien Yen: This is the incorrect spelling of the *Yen Nien* (+70) in the Eight Mansions system; you will see this mistake in many Feng Shui books.

Pa Chai: the Eight Mansions system, also spelled BaZhai.

road: A route, path, or open way for vehicles. In Feng Shui, roads are *rivers* of energy, or chi and play a huge part in analyzing a site because energy is powerful. These virtual, or urban, rivers are calculated when assessing, designing, enhancing, or implementing counter measures or enhancements for a site.

San He: Also known as *San Hup*. One of the two major schools of study in Classical Feng Shui—the other is San Yuan. The San He system, excellent for tapping natural landforms, primarily addresses large-scale projects, land plots, urban developments, city planning, and master-planned communities. The system is extensive and has several practical techniques for new and existing residential spaces as well. When assessing and altering a site or a structure, San He and San Yuan can be blended for maximum results.

San Yuan: One of the two major schools of Classical Feng Shui. The Flying Stars is part of this system; it excels in techniques of timing. See the *Schools of Feng Shui* in the compendium for more details.

sector: An area inside or outside a building: South sector, North sector, and so on.

sha chi: Also known as *shar chi*. Extremely negative energy, or killing chi.

Shan: The Chinese word for *mountain*.

Sheng Chi: Part of the Eight Mansions system. It can bring life-generating energy, wealth, and opportunities. Using Master Yap's numeric representation, this is the +90.

Shui: The Chinese word for *water*; pronounced *shway*.

sitting: In Feng Shui it refers to the back of the house, as if the structure is sitting in a chair on the land or property. It is the heavy part of the house; also consider a mountain.

Sitting Star: Also known as the Mountain Star in the Flying Star system. It influences people luck, such as fertility, employees, and health.

solar calendar: A calendar based on the movements of the sun.

Southeast Asia: Countries South of China and East of India, including Thailand, Vietnam, Cambodia, Laos, Myanmar, the Philippines, and Singapore.

Tao: also known as *The Way*, and is core of Taoism (pronounced with a D sound).

tapping the energy or chi: A technique that invites the available energy from the external environment to support the occupants of a structure.

Tien Yi: Part of the Eight Mansion system. It can bring excellent health and wealth. In Chinese it means *heavenly doctor* or *the doctor from heaven watches over you*. Using Master Yap's numeric representation, it is the +80.

tilting a door: A time-honored tradition used by Feng Shui masters and practitioners to change the degree of a door and the energy of a space. The doorframe and threshold are re-angled toward the desired degree. When the door is re-hung, it is tilted on a different degree.

T-juncture: When two roads meet perpendicularly to create a *T*. The formation is toxic when a home or business sits at the top and center of that *T*.

Traditional Feng Shui: Another term for Classical Chinese Feng Shui.

Tui: Also spelled *Dui*. One of the eight trigrams that represents the youngest daughter, the lake, and mid-fall. In the Later Heaven Ba Gua it is located in the West.

Twelve Animals: Rat, Ox, Tiger, Rabbit, Dragon, Snake, Horse, Goat, Monkey, Rooster, Dog and Pig; part of the Chinese Zodiac and used extensively in Classical Feng Shui and Chinese Astrology.

water: In Feng Shui, water is the secret to enhancing wealth, prosperity, longevity, nobility, and relationships. The Chinese word is *Shui,* and it represents energy and life force. Water, according to Feng Shui, is the most powerful element on the planet.

West Life Group: In the Eight Mansions system, people are divided into the East or West group. The 2, 6, 7, and 8 Life Guas are part of the West Life Group.

Western Feng Shui: In addition to the Black Hat Sect, other schools cropped up that incorporated the principles, but not the rituals, associated with Lin-Yun's followers. As the masters of Classical Feng Shui started to teach around the world, some of the most well-acclaimed instructors and authors of Western Feng Shui began to learn Classical Feng

Shui. Unwilling to give up the Western-style Feng Shui that made them famous, they mixed the old with the new, thereby adding to the confusion over authentic Feng Shui. More than half of the Feng Shui books written about the subject include a hodgepodge of both theories.

Wu Gwei: Part of the Eight Mansions system that can attract lawsuits, bad romance, and betrayals. Using Master Yap's numeric representation, it is the -70. This is also known as the *Five Ghosts* direction.

Wu Xing: Also known as the five elements of Feng Shui: wood, fire, earth, metal, and water.

Yang: Alive, active and moving energy; considered the male energy of the Yin-Yang symbol.

Yang Feng Shui: Feng Shui was first practiced for the selection of a perfect gravesite, or what is commonly known by the Chinese as Yin Feng Shui—Feng Shui for the dead. Later, techniques were developed to increase luck and opportunities for houses of the living.

Yen Nien: Part of the Eight Mansions system that can bring longevity, good relationships, and love. Using Master Yap's numeric representation, it is the +70. It is a common mistake to spell this term as Nen Yien.

Yin: Female energy, passive, and dead; the perfect complement is yang energy.

Xing Fa: An approach to assessing form and shape in the environment.

Xun: One of the eight trigrams of the Ba Gua, also spelled as *Sun*. It represents the eldest daughter, the wind and early summer. In the Later Heaven arrangement of the Ba Gua, the Xun trigram is located in the Southeast.

Author's Bio

Denise A. Liotta-Dennis,
Feng Shui Master, Speaker, Teacher, International Author

She's known as the "fast-talkin' Texan"—an interesting and delightful oxymoron—Denise A. Liotta-Dennis is the founder and president of Dragon-Gate Feng Shui (DGFS), LLC an international consulting and development firm, specializing in authentic Feng Shui site selection, planning, design, audits, and assessments for commercial and residential real estate and construction projects. In 2006, Denise founded The American College of Classical Feng Shui, the training arm of Dragon-Gate, a premier platform to learn Classical Feng Shui.

Born to a Houston entrepreneurial family, Denise, who possesses a quarter century of business ownership experience, is among a rare breed of Feng Shui consultants. Denise not only resonates with all things spiritual, she talks the language and walks in the shoes of business people. Growing up in the shadow of her father's construction and real estate development companies, Denise discovered early in life an innate love of business lifestyles and entrepreneurship. Her work with Feng Shui is also an outgrowth of a natural affinity for interior design. In fact, Denise has more than twenty-five years experience working in interior design, including residential and commercial projects.

With a rapid-fire delivery that keeps audiences spellbound, wide-eyed, and on the edge of their seats,

Denise—a gifted educator and speaker on Feng Shui and business topics—offers high-energy, content-rich presentations. Peppering her talks with a quaint Southwestern humor, Denise's stories are couched in the real-life foibles of entrepreneurs and those seeking a spiritual path. She shares the spiritual side of life with a practical commercial bent not found among the more esoteric practitioners common to Feng Shui.

Denise has studied with four noted Feng Shui Masters from China, Malaysia and Australia, including Grand Master Yap Cheng Hai and belongs to his 400- year Wu Chang Feng Shui Mastery lineage.

Ms Liotta-Dennis' first book was released in major national and international bookstores March 8, 2013 entitled *Classical Feng Shui for Wealth and Abundance,* her second book was released January 8, 2015 entitled *Feng Shui for Romance, Sex & Relationships,* and her third book will be released in the fall of 2016 entitled *Classical Feng Shui for Health, Beauty & Longevity* (endorsed by Grandmaster Dr. Stephen Skinner). This book has been translated into the native languages of Czechoslovakia and Estonia. She has a total of nine Feng Shui books in print.

Denise's books are sold in fine book stores in the United States, Canada, the United Kingdom, Australia, New Zealand, and Singapore. They are offered online at Walmart, Target, Barnes & Noble, Amazon, and are housed in several American libraries. International online-booksellers in Sweden, Germany, France, Poland, Japan, Italy and Denmark sell her books in English.

The American College of Classical Feng Shui (ACCFS)
Dragon Gate Feng Shui International Consultants
Master Denise Liotta Dennis
Houston, Texas USA
Phone: 713-897-1719
Email: denise@dragongatefengshui.com
Website: www.dragongatefengshui.com

Offers consulting services, books, free seminars, and training classes. There are several ways to learn more about Feng Shui. The following programs are suitable for real estate agents, architects, Feng Shui enthusiasts, interior designers, self-taught Feng Shui practitioners, builders and Feng Shui professionals seeking to deepen their knowledge, and those aspiring to a career in Feng Shui.

3-Day Intensive: Professional Certification
In this course you will learn sophisticated techniques to accurately analyze a home or business that will prepare you to be a sought-after consultant. You will learn how to simultaneously use Eight Mansions and Flying Stars, the two most important systems for interiors. Our classes are amazing, exciting and very effective, in just three days you'll know how to apply your new or years of knowledge to create impressive results. Fee: $3600

3-Day Intensive: Master Certification
The demand for skilled consultants who can produce results has far outstripped the supply. Here you will learn the most advanced techniques of Classical Feng Shui. Experienced practitioners are often hired for large projects for the development of master-planned communities, office buildings, shopping centers, hotels, and casinos. Fee: $4999

Private Mentoring: FENG SHUI MASTER Program
This is the traditional method of learning Feng Shui mastery and not for everyone. It is a 1-year program (36 Modules) taught twice a month via Skype or Zoom; Saturday or Sunday is an option if needed. The mentoring program is taught monthly and provides the most personalized, comprehensive program we offer. Contact us at denise@dragongatefengshui.com or call 713-897-1719.

How to Take a Compass Direction

Some masters take the door degree from *inside* the building. However, Grandmaster Yap taught his students to take the compass direction outside. A traditional hiking compass may vary a few degrees from a Chinese Luo Pan and a SmartPhone may vary even more. Purchase a good app that aligns with GPS as phones do not contain a magnet like a regular compass. Put your back to the door when using a phone app. It will look like the image below and give you a digital read out.

Books by
Master Denise Liotta Dennis

Printed in Great Britain
by Amazon